CONCILIUM

Religion in the Seventies

CONCILIUM

Religion in the Seventies

EDITORIAL DIRECTORS: Edward Schillebeeckx (Dogma) •
Herman Schmidt (Liturgy) • Alois Müller (Pastoral) •
Hans Küng (Ecumenism) • Franz Böckle (Moral Theology) •
Johannes B. Metz (Church and World) • Roger Aubert (Church
History) • Teodoro Jiménez Urresti (Canon Law) • Christian
Duquoc (Spirituality) • Pierre Benoît and Roland Murphy
(Scripture)

CONSULTING EDITORS: Marie-Dominique Chenu • ✠Carlo
Colombo • Yves Congar • Andrew Greeley • Jorge Mejía •
Karl Rahner • Roberto Tucci

EXECUTIVE SECRETARY: (Awaiting new appointment),
Arksteestraat 3-5, Nijmegen, The Netherlands

Volume 68: Canon Law

EDITORIAL BOARD: Teodoro Jiménez Urresti •
Peter Huizing • Manuel Bonet Muixi • Michael Breydy •
Albertus Eysink • Tomás García Barberena • Antonio García y
García • Jean Gaudemet • Johannes Gerhartz • Cornelis de Jong •
Gustav Leclerc • Gonzalez Martinez Diez • Paul Mikat •
Charles Munier • Johannes Neumann • Ladislas Örsy •
Juan Radrizzani • Giovanni Řezáč • Robert Soullard •
Luis Vela Sanchez

CONTESTATION
IN THE CHURCH

Edited by
Teodoro Jiménez Urresti

Herder and Herder

1971
HERDER AND HERDER NEW YORK
232 Madison Avenue, New York 10016

Cum approbatione Ecclesiastica

Library of Congress Catalog Card Number: 71–168654
Copyright © 1971 by Herder and Herder, Inc. and Stichting Concilium.
All rights reserved. Nothing contained in this publication shall be reproduced
and/or made public by means of print, photographic print, microfilm, or in
any other manner without the previous consent of the Stichting Concilium
and the publishers.

Printed in the United States

CONTENTS

PART II
BULLETIN

PART III
DOCUMENTATION CONCILIUM

Editorial

"CONTESTATION" is a word which brings to mind a whole series of threatening and alarming situations: street fighting against the police; attacks on government agencies, and the embassies and legations of foreign states; mass protest meetings and marches; riotous assemblies; students throwing out professors; teenage protest strikes; and a number of similar scenes and occasions. In almost every part of the world the various manifestations of established order are periodically disturbed by outbreaks of unrest, and demonstrations which are symptomatic of anxiety, uncertainty and ferment. Almost everywhere young people come forward to educate their elders and to protest against everything that their mentors hold sacred: order, law, authority, prosperity, scholarship and science, marriage and the family, and so on. And of course the ferment does not draw the line at the religious dimension of the world.

The Catholic Church is no exception; rather, the contrary is true. There is widespread evidence of a loosening-up process—which is also consciously undertaken by the Church itself; evidence too of an exodus from the existing structures of clerical organization and religious institutions; of a drop in the number of candidates for the priesthood and the orders; of the disputation of hitherto sacrosanct elements of canon law and ecclesiastical order; of conflicts between priests and bishops, and between parties within the Church; and of groups forming outside the hierarchical structure of the Church. Widespread, too, are the uncertainty and anxiety which these phenomena have evoked in traditional believers.

In such situations, to keep one's head above water means to keep a straight head. Blindly to allow oneself to succumb to anxiety and uncertainty is no more than a panic reaction. To close one's eyes to reality by taking refuge in the attitudes characterized by such judgments as "That's nothing to do with me", or "It's confined to small minorities", just as surely leads to panic once reality becomes so pressing that it can no longer be ignored.

This issue begins with a sociological analysis of the phenomenon of contestation and its typical features: more or less radical protest against the existing social order, made a-legally or illegally, by the "extra-parliamentary opposition" or outside the existing political parties; and in the Church as protest outside the existing structures, and outside the hierarchy in spontaneously formed groups, which can abandon the attempt at protest and decide to lead their own lives outside the institutional Church, deeming it past hope and even worthless—a form of protest which is a more radical challenge to the Church than contestation proper (Pin).

Of course it is impossible in this context to provide a detailed description of current forms of contestation in the Church throughout the world, but we have tried to give as proficient as possible a survey by selecting authors who can draw on relevant experience. The surveys of the situation in Western Europe (Bunnik), the United States (Philibert), Latin America (Guttierrez), Africa (van Pinxteren), Asia (Balasuriya) and Australia (Charlesworth) tend to show that inner-Church tensions are no less evident in the churches in the Socialist countries, the young churches, and the churches of the diaspora; that Vatican II, by awakening hopes for decentralization, pluriformity, collegiality, and so on, which have not—or only very inadequately—been fulfilled since then, made a major contribution to the rise of contestation; that contestation is always oriented more towards the mission of the Church in the world, and only secondarily, because of that primary direction, towards internal church relations; that consequently there is a widespread tendency for more and more laymen and non-Catholics to participate in opposition groups constituted autonomously and independently of the hierarchy; and that the original protest is increasingly becoming an active movement for the realization of positive aims. Analogous tendencies are evident in recent developments in the Evangelical churches in Federal Germany (Hasselmann).

But how is one to get these rather variegated data on contestation in the Church into some kind of just perspective? A first step in this direction is to find out what the Bible has to say on the subject. "Contestation" in the Scriptures is primarily bearing witness to the truth, supported by the Holy Spirit, in the face of unbelief. Christ himself, and the apostles and Stephen, bore witness in this sense. Biblical contestation also means protest on behalf of truth against actions which contravene truth. A typical prototype in this regard is Paul's protest against Peter (Schneider). It is reassuring to discover that there have always been situations of conflict in the course of the Church's history; and that it would be unjust and improper to make, in these instances, polar distinctions between right-thinking or legal and heretical or illegal parties. It just isn't possible to make such precise judgments on a conflict situation, which—as has been shown repeatedly—can eventually give rise to new insights and improved forms of communal life (Chenu). Even in traditional theology there are instances to support the view that ecclesiastical structures and ecclesiastical authority are always subject to the criticism of the Spirit and the Gospel (Huizing). Pope Paul VI's position on the subject of oppositional tendencies in the Church on the one hand shows clearly that fundamental values are at stake, being threatened by a veritable crisis of faith and trust. On the other hand, his judgment calls attention to the fact that the demand and striving for authenticity, truth, justice, liberation from the slavery of the consumer society, and so on, also embody fundamental values, which call Church leaders as well to a serious examination of conscience.

The bulletin on the position of the laity in Church law raises one aspect of contestation, and tends to a judgment against a one-sided clerical conception of ecclesiastical structure and organization (Lombardia). A second bulletin offers a summary account of the information available to date on the effectiveness of the papal commission concerned with the revision of canon law (Huizing).

PETER HUIZING

PART I
ARTICLES

Emile Pin

Contestation

IS contestation a modern phenomenon, or is it a new label for a perennial element in social life: dissension, negation, opposition? The second interpretation is supported by the fact that the term *"contestation"* does not exist in all languages. We find it in the languages of Latin origin—French, Italian, Spanish, Portuguese. For a more conventional English translation one hesitates between "protest", "revolt", and expressions containing the adjective "radical". In German the difficulties are similar: should we say *"Protest"* or *"Auflehnung"*? On the other hand, the Dutch are already using the word *"contestatie"*. All this seems to suggest that we should make distinctions: "contestation" is not an absolutely new phenomenon; it can be described in terms of old words; but it also implies characteristics specific to itself which suggest the introduction of a new concept.[1]

In this article, I shall try to describe characteristics specific to contestation while emphasizing the contestation of the young and the intellectuals. I shall examine how contestation differs from the other phenomena of social negation, such as making claims or demands, opposition, revolt, revolution and "dropping-out". Contestation differs from other negative actions in its aims, its methods and its protagonists.

[1] The concepts which allow us to pinpoint social phenomena are not simple abstract concepts. They are type-concepts built up from a certain number of elements which, either "ideally" or "statistically", encounter each other in the phenomenon under examination. An ideal type is one that describes either of the two poles of a typology. A statistical type is one that describes an average or a "mode".

Contestation and Claim-making

The object of demands or claims, whether these are made by an individual or a social category, is to obtain greater participation inside a determined social system, without questioning the basic values or institutions of the society or group. Claim-making presupposes integration within the social system. It rests on the conviction (whether or not this has been proved by experience) that a well-planned action will enable the desired advantage to be obtained: an increase in salaries or prices, a decrease in the hours of work, participation in decision-making, the extension of the right to vote to a new category, some modification of the law, and so on. This type of action is practised today by countless associations and unions.

Claim-making, then, is a rational sequence of actions which have as their objective the gaining of some institutional advantage. Contestation is very different, it more or less radically rejects existing institutions. It distrusts claim-making. Successful claim-making integrates its protagonists yet further within the fabric of society and strengthens the plausibility of institutions.

Claim-making can resemble contestation on the level of methods. Contestation does not respect "the rules of the game". And claim-making can also infringe the approved models of "social negation": it can express itself in the form of unauthorized public demonstrations, illegal strikes, the blocking of roads, etc. But it does not choose illegal means on principle. It chooses them by necessity, owing to the absence of other effective means, whereas illegality or a-legality is of the essence of contestation.

Claim-making is in general the action of individuals already within a network of economic or political relationships with whose working they are familiar. Contestation is usually the action of intellectuals or students who are "removed"—by situation or choice, institutionally or psychologically—from any analytical knowledge of the machinery of society.

Contestation and Opposition

The pattern of countless governmental systems is that of a majority in power confronted by a minority in opposition. This is the case with parliamentary regimes where the opposition parties are not seen as harmful to the good government of the country but as an instrument indispensable to the elaboration of good policies and good laws. Parliamentary opposition, violent though it may sometimes be, is lawful opposition and written into the institutions. Nowadays, however, another kind of opposition is developing, an extra-parliamentary opposition which does not follow any of the rules of the political game. This contestatory opposition can result in the birth of groups or movements, but these will not have a place within the spectrum of the parties. Their main difference from the other opposition parties lies not so much in their programme (although they usually produce a programme of radical negation from the point of view of institutions) as in that they refuse to play the political game. This rejection of the normal channels of opposition is equivalent to an all-embracing challenge to the institutions. A similar phenomenon occurs in the Church when a Church member addresses himself to authority by means of the mass media, instead of making use of the—very vague—channels that exist to let authority know a divergent point of view. Such procedure is of a contestatory type, even if the protest is not all-embracing in its content; it remains so in its form. The proof lies in the shock experienced by authority. Such conduct is then described as irresponsible, impertinent, even malicious, whatever the dignity or rank of the person involved. It is then said—not without some hypocrisy— that there were other ways of airing the divergent point of view.[2] This means "legal" ways, ways approved by the group. This would be true, up to a point, in a parliamentary system. It would be difficult to prove it in a hierarchical and authoritarian system like that of the Catholic Church, where all opposition which is not secret and not expressed through official channels becomes a rupture of discipline, a contestation. Here again it can be seen that contestation is not necessarily all-embracing in its content; it can bear on one precise point only, but it is all-embracing in its methods, for it does not express itself according to the rules; it shows a contempt for the rules, and this in a very self-conscious

[2] One of the most striking examples is the Instruction elaborated by the Congregation of the Council and sent out by the Holy Office to all the bishops concerning the status of priests who have reverted to the lay estate. This Instruction was worked out in secret by the Roman Curia some months before the Synod of Bishops (which represents a first and very cautious form of democratic participation) could discuss it!

way; and it rejects in advance the reproach of not having followed the normal paths of communication. Nevertheless contestation possesses elements in common with opposition. Both the one and the other operate essentially through the spoken word. But in one case the word is permitted, even required, whereas the contestatory word is a word usurped by force. This also suggests that contestation presupposes in its instigator a sufficiency of power within the social system: the grown-up son at home, the high-up functionary in administration, the prelate or theologian in the Church, or again a relatively sizeable mass of individuals, as was the case in Paris in May 1968: not power guaranteed by law, but power possessed by the individual or the category owing to the weight (recognized competence, social position, acclaim of the masses) of which they dispose in society.

Contestation, Revolt, Rebellion

Contestation probably has more affinity with revolt or rebellion than with any other form of social negation. Revolt by a category or a group of dissatisfied men (an unjustly-treated category like slaves, serfs, artisans, or a minority group such as a conquered race or a neglected province) is one of the simplest and most primitive forms of negation. Unlike revolutionary or reformist action, revolt and rebellion do not presuppose a detailed analysis of the existing situation. They arise from discontent, from a conviction of being unjustly discriminated against. They are violent. Revolt is directed less against systems of social organization than against men. Revolt may well conceal a vague desire for a more just society; but, if it succeeds, the rebels often reproduce—but to their own advantage—the only type of society they have known, an oppressive type of society. The only thing that differentiates it from the past is that it is not the same individuals that oppress or are oppressed.

The way in which contestation most resembles revolt is in its all-embracing, non-analytical characteristics. Contestation—that is to say, radical contestation—does not go in for detailed examination of the elements that make up contemporary society; it does not patiently take the machinery to pieces; it does not make a study of the juridical and economic complexities that might explain the existing pattern of basic relationships between men; in what it calls "the system" or "the establishment" it is incapable of distinguishing between elements linked together by essential relationships and characteristics that are purely accidental. Everything is rejected *en bloc*. It will be said that all this is applicable only to all-embracing contestation. True; but, as I said earlier, all contestation is potentially total because it rejects the rules of the game.

Nevertheless contestation differs from revolt and rebellion in two essential ways:

1. To a greater or lesser degree, contestation is aware of the dangers for a future society of reproducing the errors of the existing society. In this sense contestation is post-revolutionary. But unlike revolutionary projects, contestation does not offer—at least in its initial phases—a new model of society. Contestation is as dissatisfied with Socialist societies, as they exist today, as with liberal societies. Contestation is opposed to the phenomenon of institutionalism itself. It hopes for a new type of society of which it has a somewhat vague picture but where friendship, equality and mutual esteem will reign. Unlike the rebel, the contestator does not want to reproduce—but to his own advantage—the old model of social repression, and yet his indifference regarding institutional reorganization risks in practice being translated into a new domination.

2. The other aspect distinguishing the contestator from the rebel relates to methods. As the rebel has a specific aim—that of taking over the lawful power—he does not hesitate to make use of the only way open to him: namely, violence. The contestator uses the word, the word of negation, the word of contempt. He wants no truck with a power which he knows he would be incapable of exercising and which would compel him to create new institutions. So the contestator cannot push his project through to the end. He protests, rejects, but offers no precise solution, so does not throw himself into organized action—whether violent or peaceful—in order to seize power. However, this does not mean that his "word" is ineffective. The authorities—of the nation or organization in which contestation breaks out—cannot for ever ignore the phenomenon; they feel compelled, often belatedly, to seek the causes of this "impertinent" protest.

Contestation, Revolution and Anarchy

At first sight, the concepts of revolution and contestation seem very close, and it is probable that the two attitudes are often found in the same person. Yet there is a distinction to be made between them. The revolutionary attitude is more ancient than contestation. It consists in rejecting existing society in the name of another idea of social organization. From Plato to Marx and Mao Tse Tung, mankind has seen countless revolutionary projects; utopias form one class. The revolutionary, unlike the rebel or the contestator, is a theorist who, having analysed contemporary society and hopefully discovered the root of contemporary social evils, reconstructs the society of tomorrow on new principles. This is the case with Marxism, which discovered that the exploitation of man by man was attributable to the private ownership of the means of production, and therefore builds an ideal future society on the collective appropriation of capital. The revolutionary wants radical change; "radical" means that, having found the principle or principles which lie at the root of the evil, he feels himself able to build a totally different society. The revolutionary is not a reformist who wants to rearrange society, nor a rebel who wants to take over power himself out of revenge, but a radical and disinterested saviour of humanity. It is not by these two last characteristics that he differs from the contestator. He differs in that he possesses a precise plan of social reconstruction based on an analysis of social systems.

This is what makes revolution "serious", whereas the contestatory word is rarely voiced by "reasonable people", people involved in the mechanics of social interaction, people who are informed. The serious adult accuses the contestator of "not really knowing the thing against which he inveighs", of "not knowing the complexity and subtlety of the mechanism that makes life between men possible. It is the fruit of age-long experiment", the serious adult goes on; "if you want to destroy everything you will produce a primordial chaos from which mankind will probably never extricate itself." And this is true. One of the features of the contestation of the intellectuals and the young is the conceptual poverty of their language (whether concerning history, law, economics or politics). The abhorred enemy is, in turn, "the system", "the establishment", "the consumer society", "capitalism" (within which last all contemporary forms of society are arbitrarily ranged, including the Soviet and sometimes even the Chinese!).

It is not easy to explain how students, when over twenty, or teachers, when over forty, as most of them are, can give themselves so easily to such intellectual bacchanalia. The main causes are, it seems to me, the growing complexity of the machinery of society, the partitioning-off of social sectors, a system of education that isolates teachers and students from the rest of society and prevents them from taking part in the economic adventure, the prolongation of the period of preparation which obliges more and more young people to live in insecurity and uncertainty when their biological, affective and intellectual powers have already reached their peak. To all this should be added the relative but growing importance that these young people have within the total population.

All this explains the noise, the vigour, but also the absence of content in youthful and intellectual contestation. It could be called revolutionary, but not in the sense accorded to revolutionary action up till now—something serious, scientific, even dogmatic. Another difference between revolution and contestation lies in the means employed. The revolutionary does not normally demur at resorting to violence. Convinced that he can build a better world, he does not hesitate to use means for which, perhaps, he has little sympathy but which seem to him the indispensable price to pay for the freeing of mankind.

Anarchy, on the other hand, combines the characteristics of contestation and revolution: the anarchist wants to turn the existing social order upside-down and this by violent means. He is prepared to unleash "total subversion". But he does not want to build up any predetermined society. He wants total suppression of power, of institutions, of the police. In this he approximates to the contestator. Their difference lies in their methods of action. The contestator gives himself to a symbolic destruction of the social order; the anarchist is prepared to take up arms.

Contestation and "Dropping-out"

All the phenomena of negation studied so far are concerned with existing society so as to reform it, change it or reject it. But the people expressing these various forms of negation normally continue to live at the heart of the society they have denied. This is especially true of many contestators who, while rejecting "the system", nevertheless live off it. The phenomenon that we call "dropping-out" seems much more peaceful, though basically it is more radical. It consists of an individual or a group organizing their existence outside the system of officially-approved social relationships: monks in the desert, tramps and vagabonds, certain rural sects like the Doukhobors, the Protestant Reformation, bohemians, hippie groups, the "underground church"—all are examples of "dropping-out". The people belonging to these groups have lost, whether temporarily or permanently, any hope that society or the organization (for instance, the institutional Catholic Church) can provide an acceptable framework for life. So in their eyes it is useless to protest, to contest, and still more useless to try to make claims or reforms. The "drop-out" has done all that, but—in his view—in vain: he has achieved nothing. His word has fallen on deaf ears, or beaten against intractable obstacles obstructing the system of communication. So why not ignore the system, behave as if it didn't exist, arrange things just for himself? The rebel and the revolutionary take over the strong-holds of power, the contestator has recourse to the word, but the "drop-out" falls silent, disappears, goes to earth. The only response he can make to the institution that angers him is a smile and a shrug of the shoulders. At the most he will say with Christ: "Let the dead bury their dead."

"Dropping-out" makes no noise. But it is a more formidable enemy to institutions than contestation. Contestation can be re-absorbed in two ways: spontaneously, as when the contestator who has no programme lets himself be reintegrated within the institutional system; and in an organized way, as when the high-ups in the social system give place to the opposition within the system itself. But authoritarian and hierarchical systems do not admit of such internal opposition; so they prefer the reintegration of contestators, or, alternatively, an "excommunication" which in their eyes should be equivalent to civil death. But even before ex-communication is pronounced, the contestator who does not want to submit could have elected to "drop out". And against "dropping-out" the authorities have only the meagre weapons of irrational force; unless they prefer to shut their eyes, or unless institutional isolation has prevented them from even seeing what has happened. "Dropping-out" can form the basis of a new culture. "Dropping-out" is creative.

*   *   *   *

Contestation is not a simple phenomenon. It can take many forms. In its content it oscillates between rejection of a partial aspect of the social system, and all-embracing or total rejection. But even when contestation is aimed at some particular point it still retains its all-embracing character, either because the precise object of reform is only part of an overall criticism of the existing state of things, or (and perhaps more importantly) because contestation is a "taking-over of the word", a "usurpation of the word" outside the normal channels of claims and opposition. In its methods contestation constitutes an all-embracing challenge, and an infringement of the rules of the game. In the eyes of authority, contestation is adolescent, impertinent, ill-timed. Contestation is not based on any detailed analysis of the machinery of society, so that the contestator's rejection seems to show either plain ignorance of the constraints inherent in every society, or frank contempt for the rules in force. However, such contempt is not total. Contestation pays institutions the compliment of recognizing their existence and their weight; it shows a certain acquaintance with the utterances of authority. "Dropping-out" goes a step further. "Drop-outs" have already set to work to give birth to a new society. Their contempt for existing society can be much more radical and at the same time more peaceful. After all, there's no point in fighting the dead. It is better silently to take the path of a new life.

Translated by Barbara Wall

Ruud J. Bunnik

Common-purpose Groups in Western Europe

I. General Features

THIS article is concerned with groups of Christians who, since about 1968, have been working in almost every Western European country with the aim of renewing the Church consistently and radically. I prefer to avoid the word "contestation", partly because it does not sufficiently stress the positive aim of these groups—to make the Christian message function better in the modern world—and partly because there are also other "contestation" groups which oppose all renewal in the Church, as well as "official" groups of bishops and theologians who contest the slow pace of renewal.

These critical, common-purpose groups are distinguished by their extra-parliamentary or para-canonical character. They have not been officially instituted, or recognized formally. They have arisen quite spontaneously because of dissatisfaction with the official Church's slowness or indifference with regard to concrete renewal. They first appeared in 1968 or thereabouts, a few years after the close of Vatican II, when many Christians were beginning to suspect that renewal was not being taken seriously enough, that many aspects of it would simply be forgotten and that it was generally threatened by caution, a fear of real freedom and reaction in the Church.

The causes of this suspicion are well known. In the universal Church, the principle of collegiality was not being seriously applied. Pluriformity was hardly recognized. Injustice, war and poverty received inadequate attention. The encyclicals *Humanae*

Vitae and *Sacerdotalis celibatus* appeared and the renewal of theology and catechetics was obstructed. At the local level, there was insufficient collegial co-operation between bishops and their priests. Fear of difficulties with Rome still prevented bishops from encouraging active renewal. The critical groups rejected this timidity and insisted that the living Church had to change at least partly as the result of local experiment and not as the result of reforms imposed from above.

The groups have developed remarkably in the few years that they have been in existence. At first they consisted mainly of priests, partly because of the pressing problems of clerical status, obligatory celibacy, and so on. These problems had to be solved if the Church was to be credible and to contribute effectively to the removal of violence and injustice from the world. Quite soon, however, the element of "trade unionism" which the movement featured at the beginning became more broadly political, and lay Catholics and even non-Catholics joined it.

The members of these groups are not humanists working for a better world, but committed Christians, convinced that the ultimate meaning and salvation of the better world are to be found in the God of Israel and his son Jesus. In this total commitment, they are hindered and frustrated by much in the traditional Church. They are not sectarian and do not feel drawn to an "underground" Church, because they are convinced that only powerful, united and coherent Christian action can successfully renew the face of the earth. They do, however, distinguish between active Christianity and traditional membership of the institution of the Church. They question the absolute value of existing structures and laws, and regard orthopraxis and unity with the underprivileged as more important than orthodoxy and the unity of Church discipline.

Mistrust and even conflict are, of course, frequent results. As always, the fault is on both sides. The groups have in many cases still to find the right positive formulas and the most convincing tactics. The "official" Church, on the other hand, sometimes accepts these groups as serious partners in dialogue, but more often only has contact with them in an exchange of written protests and condemnations.

II. A SURVEY OF THE EXISTING GROUPS

I confine myself here to those groups which have more than a simply local or parochial importance and which are, for the most part, in contact with the international secretariat of the *Assemblée Internationale des Chrétiens Solidaires* in Louvain. So little information is available about similar groups in Eastern Europe that these have to be excluded.

1. *Belgium*

The linguistic division in Belgian society and the conservative attitude of many of the Belgian bishops mean that Christian renewal there is slow and cautious. The bishops' reaction to *Humanae Vitae* was extremely vague. Although they are in principle in favour of ordaining married men, priests who marry have no future in any field in which the Church is influential (they cannot, for example, become lay teachers). The Walloon critical groups are united in *Présence et Témoignage* and are in close contact with French groups. Two important Flemish groups are the *Federatie van Vlaamse Universiteitsparochies* and the *Open Vergadering van Westvlaamse Priesters*. Two other groups, *Inspraak* and *Exodus,* have achieved some notoriety because of their campaign for a more humane treatment of married priests. A great deal of renewal takes place within or in collaboration with the official organizations, but many critical Catholics believe that it is going ahead far too slowly.

2. *Great Britain*

The Roman Catholic Church in Great Britain is a social minority with a rather inward-looking attitude and is led by bishops who are almost all conservative and paternalistic. There were sharp reactions to the departure of Charles Davis and the dismissal from *New Blackfriars* of Herbert McCabe in 1966–1967, but very few to the encyclical on priestly celibacy. *Humanae Vitae*, on the other hand, and the resulting suspension of a number of diocesan priests who spoke out against it, caused a great deal of unrest.

The Catholic Renewal Movement has about three thousand members, most of them lay people, and was formed in the first place to co-ordinate opposition to *Humanae Vitae*. The movement published a brochure in August 1970, once again rejecting the official attitude towards birth regulation. The bishops' reaction was moderate, but they were clearly not in favour of accepting the movement's representatives as partners in dialogue. Since its creation, the movement has widened its aims considerably, to include, for example, celibacy, the liturgy and lay participation.

There are many Catholics in the more recent, ecumenical group One for Christian Renewal. The Catholic New Left dates from 1963—its journal, *Slant*, is no longer published—and its members are sympathetic towards Marxist ideas and are rather cool in their attitude towards the present plans for renewal, which they believe are not radical enough.

The hitherto very bad contact between bishops and priests in Britain may eventually be improved as a result of the Wood Hall Conference (June 1970) of priests from all dioceses, at which radical views were expressed, above all by priests from Liverpool. So far, however, little help is available for priests and religious whose lives have reached a critical point.

3. *France*

The French bishops, supported by a secretariat which is often haughty in its attitude and theologically reactionary, are placed between the two poles of an extreme conservatism led by a small group of prominent and very vocal Catholics and an equally extreme but diverse renewal movement. The reaction to the contestation of the workers and students in 1968 was so cautious that it seemed as though the Church was in favour of the old order.

In late 1968, about two hundred priests expressed their views about celibacy and secular work at a meeting in Lyons. This was followed by a circular letter containing more demands. Five hundred signatures were received. In January and June 1969, two further meetings led to the formation of *Échanges et dialogue*, with its two primary aims of radically renewing the status of the clergy and of social and political solidarity with the underprivileged. The bishops also met twice in 1969 to discuss the problems of the priesthood, with few concrete results, and published, in June 1970, a long document on renewal which was criticized by *Échanges et dialogue* as expressing the "new dogma of the infallibility of the French bishops". At the beginning of 1970, the secretariat of the episcopate had said that the thousand members of *Échanges et dialogue* did not satisfy the conditions of a genuine search for truth.

Another united, critical group, formed from many local groups in 1969, and less concerned with the problems of the priesthood, is *Concertation*. The *Association des prêtres mariés* exists mainly to look after the interests of married priests who are not cared for by the official Church.

4. *Italy*

The Italian bishops are mostly extremely conservative and their Church, strictly controlled by the Roman Curia and characterized by an almost magical sacramental practice and by individualistic piety, still stands aloof from the great Italian problem of social and economic inequality. From time to time, individual Christians and small groups—for example, in Parma, Florence (Isolotto), Turin (Vandalino) and Ravenna—protest against the Church's abuse of power. There are many small renewal groups in contact with each other, but so far no national organization exists.

5. *The Netherlands*

Here the bishops are not isolated, the theologians are competent, and the Church is well organized. Discussion about the Church's future began immediately after Vatican II. The greatest achievement of all, perhaps, was the Pastoral Council (six sessions, 1968–1970).

The point of departure was priestly celibacy. The Dutch bishops knew that the law had to be changed, but chose the cautious "long way". In December 1968, a united, critical group of originally seventy priests (the *Septuagint* group) insisted, however, that married clergy should be allowed to remain fully active as priests. In February 1969, this group placed their demand within a much wider context of renewal, sending a letter to all Dutch priests about authority in the Church, marriage, intercommunion and many other subjects. In March 1969, a programme of energetic social commitment entitled "Growth towards Critical and Active Communities" was published and is now being worked out in practice.

Septuagint now has more than two thousand members, including a number of "critical" Jesuits and Reformed ministers. It is recognized as the representative body of most Dutch Christians whose aim is renewal, and its criticism of the official Church in the Netherlands is now often confined simply to the tactics of renewal.

6. *Spain and Portugal*

The main problem here, of course, is the close link between the Church and the political dictatorship. The governments of both countries are active in "protecting" the Church against all attempts at renewal which might lead to a social and political commitment. All means of "protection" are regarded as suitable —secret police, arrests, political trials and the active encouragement of Catholics who are opposed to renewal. The largely conservative episcopate reacts either not at all or else only half-heartedly to this. The criticism of "contestation" groups is directed more against the official Church's complicity in various forms of oppression than against the very slow pace of renewal in the Church.

The negative attitude of the State and the Church, the ban on public meetings (for example, in Avila in June 1970), and the intensely regional feelings all make it very difficult for local groups to be organized into a national movement. At present, however, there is some federal co-operation between Spanish and Portuguese groups.

7. *Western Germany, Austria and Switzerland*

The first really large-scale signs of contestation were apparent at the Katholikentag in Essen in September 1968—keen opposition to *Humanae Vitae*, strong support for the Dutch Catechism and an urgent appeal for free speech in the Church, made clearly to the German bishops, the more conservative of whom want above all to control all developments themselves.

The various critical groups of priests received publicity in May 1968 when they announced that they were going to hold an opinion poll about celibacy. This was strongly disapproved of by the German bishops, who had so far done nothing about this problem themselves. A year later, the association of German priests, the *Arbeitsgemeinschaft von Priestergruppen in der Bundesrepublik Deutschland*, was set up and there are now more than twenty-five branches, some with lay members, with regular national assemblies, studying, discussing and taking action on the priesthood, the election of bishops, mixed marriages, the national synod, the relationship between Church and State, and help for developing countries. Other groups are the *Paulusgesellschaft*, the *Bensberger Kreis* and the *Lorscheidgruppe*, all of which are orientated towards society, and the extreme group known as *Kritischer Katholizismus*. Similar critical and united groups can be found in Austria and Switzerland.

III. The Three International Congresses

The Dutch *Septuagint* group suggested in the spring of 1969 that the common-purpose critical groups in different countries should meet regularly to exchange information and ideas. The first step was the setting up of a provisional secretariat for the newly formed *Assemblée européenne des prêtres* and arrangements for a first congress.

1. *Chur (5–10 July 1969)*
The problem of the priesthood was prominent on the agenda of the second symposium of Western European bishops at Chur (7–10 July 1969), and, as contacts between bishops and priests were so poor in so many countries, the inevitable question in the minds of many critical priests was, what was the point of discussing their problem if they were not there? Chur, then, was the obvious choice for the first congress, and the priests went there in the hope that contact would be made with the bishops, who were therefore asked beforehand, and again in Chur, to receive a deputation from the *Assemblée européenne*. Partly because they thought that the *Assemblée* was not representative, the bishops, however, refused, thereby depriving themselves of an opportunity to learn what the priests were really experiencing, thinking and demanding. What is more, the episcopal conference itself failed because it was too theoretical and not

properly presented to the press. This reinforced the general impression that the bishops either did not really understand the problems confronting their priests or else were afraid to talk about them openly.

The priests' meetings, on the other hand, were public and, generally speaking, efficiently conducted, and produced positive results. Attitudes towards celibacy and the priest's social commitment and possible secular employment were clarified. The functioning of the episcopal office was also discussed, and a letter was sent to the Pope calling for a radical renewal of the Church and of offices in the Church. The reaction of the press was generally favourable, while the bishops' isolation was regretted.

While in Chur, the priests decided to meet again in Rome when the bishops met there in synod in the autumn. Their theme of "free the Church so that it can free the world" went much farther than the problem of the Church and the priestly office. In a circular letter, the priests declared: "We are going to Rome because we regard the synod as extremely important. The life and growth of the local churches are at stake. We want to help the bishops to implement the decrees of Vatican II."

2. *Rome (10–16 October 1969)*

The priests were not welcomed in Rome. Only the Waldensian community offered them accommodation, and the Congregation for the Clergy tried to take the wind out of their sails by organizing a meeting of the presidents of the bishops' conferences with some of their priests.

The "Red Book" and very many other texts formed the basis for discussion, which was open to the press, but was very difficult because of the large agenda and the many participants (about 125 priests). All the same, the final texts on such subjects as the local churches, the Pope, the role of the bishop, the Church in the world and the priest in the Church were concise and clear. One draft text ("Possession, Power and Ideology"), although not an official declaration, none the less clearly reflects the priests' objections to the present sociological structure of the Church.

The priests requested a special audience with the Pope, but this was refused, partly because they were not thought to be representative, and because some of them were in conflict with their superiors. Most of the theologians who were in contact with them did not find it difficult to recognize the legitimacy of the critical groups. One contact with the bishops in Rome is worth mentioning—a conversation between the *Septuagint* group and Cardinal Alfrink led to a strongly-worded intervention on the following day (15 October) by the Cardinal at the otherwise unimpressive consultation with the Congregation for the Clergy.

At the close of their congress, the priests of the *Assemblée européenne* went to the *Confessio Petri* to express their loyalty to the Church. It can safely be said that their presence at Chur and at Rome contributed to a fuller recognition of the problem of the priesthood. It is to be hoped that their views will be heard at the bishops' synod in 1971.

3. *Amsterdam (28 September–3 October 1970)*

The third congress differed in several important respects from the previous two meetings. At least one-fifth of the participants were lay people, and many non-Catholic Christians took part. The name of the movement was changed to *Assemblée internationale des Chrétiens solidaires* and the theme of the congress—"The Church in Society"—is clear evidence that the members did not want to restrict their thinking simply to Church matters. There were more than 350 participants from more than thirty countries, not only Western Europe.

This enormous growth caused difficulties. There were so many different problems and attitudes that it was not easy to make the idea of solidarity and unity a living reality. One thought, however, tended to predominate—the failure of the Church in modern society. The resulting question was inevitably, was it not a waste of time to try to patch it up if so much of its essentially Christian fabric had been worn out?

In so far as the congress achieved any united viewpoint, it was that "the" Church and "society" as such were too abstract to be renewed and that the whole Church and the whole of society were best served by everyone renewing them locally. International contacts could help by providing moral support and by making joint declarations against abuses, injustice, and so on, and it is in this light that the resolutions passed by the congress on the violation of human rights in Spain and Brazil, the exploitation of immigrant workers in Europe, the concordats between the Church and States, curial and episcopal dictatorship, and the inhuman treatment of married priests should be seen.

Two other facts are worth mentioning in connection with this brief account to the Amsterdam congress. Two Dutch bishops took part for the first time. The motion on oppression in the Church, which did not obtain a majority at the congress of theologians at Brussels in September 1970, was passed in Amsterdam with an overwhelming majority.

IV. Conclusion

In a letter read by Cardinal Suenens at the bishops' meeting at Chur, Hans Küng warned that "the renewal would be continued with the bishops or without them and if necessary against them. This", Küng said, "would be disastrous. Both priests and lay people are now no longer following not only the Pope but also the bishops in many ways and there is an ever-widening 'credibility gap' between the bishops on the one hand and priests and lay people on the other."

Many people are wondering nowadays whether the "official" Church, and especially the bishops' college, is in fact capable and courageous enough to renew the Church and the world consistently, radically and effectively. The emergence of united critical groups is, as it were, writing on the wall. Only the future will tell us whether the will to renewal manifested by these groups will be taken seriously and used by the Church as a whole or whether it will simply be quietly suppressed. Above all, our bishops must cease to be indifferent to, distrustful of, and even hostile to the united groups of priests and lay people, who are patient, but will not wait for ever.

In this article, I have made extensive use of the records and publications of the *Septuagint* group and of recent material in *Informations Catholiques Internationales, Herder Korrespondenz* and *Katholiek Archief/ Archief der Kerken*.

Translated by David Smith

Paul Philibert

Dissent and Protest in the American Church

THE unexpected phenomenon of dissent in the American Church has erupted from the frustrated desires of theologically-minded Catholics seeking to live the Christian life according to the fullness suggested by the ecclesiology of Vatican II and the thought of twentieth-century European theologians. Constructing a schema of the types of protest at work here will clarify the meaning of the past decade of turbulence. Three categories suggest themselves.

I. TYPES OF PROTEST

1. *Protest denouncing Policies of Clear Injustice or Prejudice*

A radical minority here believe that unless the Catholic Church can identify itself as a maker of peace and an agent of change in a world threatened by social injustice and ecological ruination, its gospel preaching will be empty chatter. Fathers Daniel and Philip Berrigan are the best-known of these dissenters. Their dramatic protests against the American War in Vietnam constitute a prophetic challenge to American consciences. The Berrigans' struggle to elicit a national resolve to turn against war is clearly motivated by a belief that the Church is obliged to lead the way in that change.

Earlier, Catholic participation in the 1965 Civil Rights march at Selma, Alabama (where clergymen of all faiths came to support Southern Blacks in their demands for equal voting rights) marked a turning-point. Television and newspaper coverage dramatized the presence of priests and nuns marching in the lines of protesters, many of them present despite the opposition of their Ordinaries and of the bishop of the place. After Selma, the country knew that there was a cadre of American Catholics who felt conscience-bound to make their voices heard in the name of social justice.

2. *Affirmation of Rights in the Face of Repressive Legislation or Teaching*

The formation of a number of priests' associations has followed a disillusionment with the token gestures of many bishops, some of whom hand-picked the members of their diocesan priests' senate. The Association of Chicago Priests, the strongest of these groups, banded together without seeking the approval of their archbishop and, despite ups and downs, have proven themselves a serious voice in favour of honest change. The National Federation of Priests' Councils has sought to provide national strength for many weaker organizations in other dioceses.

But, of course, a far more significant and serious problem is the response to *Humanae Vitae*, the encyclical of Paul VI on birth control. The most concerted opposition within the Church to this absolute condemnation of artificial contraception came from American theologians.

The day following the publication of *Humanae Vitae*, Professor Charles Curran and nineteen associates at the Catholic University of America in Washington, together with some other priests, issued to the press a statement dissenting from the papal teaching. The topic of birth control had been much discussed just before the appearance of the encyclical: the liberal views of certain Dutch theologians were already commonly known throughout the country.[1] But since a strong liberal opinion on birth control was limited generally to an élite in universities and seminaries, the statement of Curran and the others must be seen as a pastoral attempt to prevent, on the one hand, the rigidifying

---

[1] The majority and minority reports of the papal birth control commission were published by the *National Catholic Reporter* in April 1967. The release of this documentation had considerable influence in forming the consciences of many Catholics.

of the consciences of simple Catholics and to retain, on the other hand, the allegiance of better-educated American Catholics.

The Archbishop of Washington responded to the statement by suspending the priests of his diocese who were involved, and by calling for the suspension of the Catholic University professors from academic functions. These professors have since been reinstated to teaching by the University. Of the sixty-one priests of the diocese who signed, seventeen withdrew their signatures during interviews with Cardinal O'Boyle. Of the others, over twenty have left the ministry and nineteen still remain without faculties.

The *Humanae Vitae* issue has scarred the American Church. One of the participants in the struggle has characterized the attitude of both sides of the issue as that proper to jungle warfare. The Cardinal maintained throughout an authoritarian and simplistic stance: in his mind the encyclical was "the law of God" and the matter was closed for good.

It appears that Curran's dissent has achieved a decisive influence. The majority of theologians in the U.S.A. have taken a similar position for pastoral reasons. Although a definitive moral teaching about birth control is still lacking, there exists, at least in the universities, a large base of dissent from the papal encyclical with a consequent influence upon the pastoral practice of most of the younger clergy.

3. *The Quiet Elaboration of New Modes of Behaviour which respond to Felt Needs*

The appearance of the *National Catholic Reporter*, a lay-edited Catholic weekly newspaper, in the early days of Vatican II is a good example. Traditionally, Catholic newspapers in the past simply concealed controversial or unfavourable news. *N.C.R.* chose to deal openly with controversy, with scandal, and with the human failings of Catholics. As a result, the paper has served as a social conscience on many issues of great importance, making accessible to the nation perspectives and information otherwise unavailable. This contribution has served to demolish the cloak-and-dagger secrecy which characterized ecclesiastical controversy in the past and has made it possible for diocesan papers to be more open in these matters.

Alongside the liberation of the Catholic press, a movement of quiet dissent has been spreading (one area of this dissent is frequently called "the underground Church": liturgical and communal groupings which consider themselves freed of the norms of canonical legislation). There are various manifestations of this functional dissent. Some religious and diocesan clergy, for example, seek the privacy and the autonomy of a home or an apartment in place of a rectory or a convent. Among lay Christians, too, there is a decreasing participation in the parish liturgy, especially among the young: the absence of those between eighteen and thirty-five years of age is conspicuous in many urban parishes. In addition, large numbers of religious and priests have left the ecclesiastical structures. Recent studies indicate that the stability of commitment to religious vocations here is increasingly precarious.

A very public example of dissent in the evolution of new forms is the case of the Immaculate Heart of Mary Sisters of Los Angeles. This congregation of religious women up-dated their constitutions in a general chapter of 1967. The changes include wearing non-distinctive dress, local government by consensus, an horarium chosen by the individual houses of religious according to their needs, and a choice of ministry other than the education of the young. Cardinal McIntyre, then Archbishop of Los Angeles, dismissed the Sisters from their positions in Catholic schools of the diocese and his intervention led to the summoning of an apostolic visitator to judge their behaviour. The entire incident received much coverage in the press. The Cardinal refused to accede to the Sisters' terms of renewal, while the Sisters remained determined to abide by the legislation of their chapter. This case closed with the large majority of the I.H.M. Sisters leaving public religious life in the Church to re-group as an association freed of legal obligations to Rome. There are several smaller groups of religious women who, like the I.H.M. Sisters, are searching for a life of gospel fraternity outside the jurisdiction of the Holy See. The successful transition of a large community of women religious from "inside" to "outside" ecclesiastical jurisdiction may well prove an attractive alternative to dedicated Christians at this time when Church administrators exercise an immense amount of unstructured and uncontrolled discretion.[2]

II. THE INTERPRETATION OF DISSENT

The past decade has irreversibly changed the Catholic experience in the U.S.A. Within this period, public dissent has played an important role in re-situating Catholic consciousness outside the ghetto-mentality of an immigrant Church. The loyalty of the ghetto is gone; a new honesty marks the present. Some still dream of returning to the security and tranquillity which existed before Vatican II. Others guess that the U.S. may be in the vanguard of the future, struggling towards a sociological answer to the question of the Church's existence in an automated, technologized society. Neither position is likely to be satisfied very soon, for the signs are that neither a return to the past nor a definitive option for the future is very close on the horizon. The struggle is likely to continue for another generation. Certain needs are clear, however, and these needs do allow for corrective action.

The respected historian, John Tracy Ellis, sees a need for a new style of relationships within the Church based on "participation" and "free exchange of ideas". He sees "the failure of far too many of [the Church's] spokesmen to be open and honest" as "the most damaging single defect in the Church in this country".[3] Yet he warns against a developing spirit of activism. Ellis comments that horizontal activism, whether as a fight for justice or as a campaign for renewal, cannot satisfy the deepest need of contemporary man for transcendent meaningfulness. In the light of Vatican II's call to holiness, an age of activism would be a terrible impoverishment of the renewing Church.

Another commentary on the current scene comes closer to the

[2] These examples are illustrative rather than exhaustive. Many other incidents could be mentioned. And, of course, some activity of dissent does exist on "the Right" as well as these examples from "the Left" (e.g., a growing number of pastors and laymen are protesting the experience-centred, post-kerygmatic style of catechesis predominant now in the American Church). The incidents mentioned here, however, do illustrate a certain topography of the spirit of dissent in the U.S.

[3] J. T. Ellis, "Whence Did They Come, These Uncertain Priests of the 1960's?", *Amer. Eccles. Review* 162 (1970), pp. 165-6.

global problem of dissent. T. Steeman sees the rigidity of the bishops as a key: "There have been changes in values, norms, life goals, and in the understanding of the core ritual in the community of the faithful, which are not accepted by the hierarchy."[4] The American layman has broadened his vision; the bishop has not. Catholics have been taught by Vatican II that the layman has full status as a member of the People of God. They have likewise been taught that the Church understands itself in this day as a serving community, open to the needs and anguish of the world.

Steeman suggests that too many American bishops are less inspired by this conciliar perspective than they are by lingering attitudes of an immigrant Church. The American Church came to a country already Protestant, to meet with open Protestant hostility. In addition to its own understandable defensiveness, the American Church's few moments of brilliant leadership in the nineteenth and early twentieth centuries were always threatened by the cloud of Roman resistance to any suspicion of "Americanism". The Catholic school system in America represents the building of an alternative culture, a bastion of defence against the culture of the majority.

III. The Spirit of the Dissent

The spirit which informs much of the dissent in the American Church is revealed in a comment of Rosemary Reuther: "Sooner or later one wakes up to the fact that one does not have a Sunday obligation to destroy one's soul." She laments a parish celebration so little imbued with either the spirit of the Gospel or with the spirit of life as to be depressing and destructive of the faith proclaimed in the assembly. This complaint indicates the presence in our midst of Christians who find themselves conscience-bound to demand greater authenticity in experiences which go by the name of *Christian*.

The experience in question may be the parish celebration of the liturgy, a public utterance by a bishop, or the demand that a

---

[4] T. Steeman, "The Underground Church: The Forms and Dynamics of Change in Contemporary Catholicism", *The Religious Situation 1969*, ed. D. Cutler (Boston, 1969), p. 719.

community of religious react according to patterns characteristic of primary relationships in group living. Whatever the case, the dissenting minority interprets its dissent not only as self-defence, but also as a kind of witness, testifying to the inadequacies of existing forms and to the demands of the changing times. In extreme cases, this discontent rejects the Church's claim to a gospel mandate, as does Miss Reuther, who calls the official Church "merely a faction within those who call themselves Christian".

IV. A PARADOX OF LEADERSHIP

The American Church badly lacks true pastoral and theological leadership at this moment. Meanwhile, some answer must be given to those who reject the Church's public worship and its social conscience in the name of a more authentic fidelity to the Gospel. Many of those more experienced in life and in administration are no longer available to contribute their talents. Older people are terribly frightened. They see the young no longer praying, released from past moral restraints and asceticism, and experiencing serious problems of faith. As a result, old people retreat into seclusion, seeking security from the past. Brilliant exceptions exist, of course; but most of the older churchmen are lost as leaders.

On the other hand, the dissenters are frequently persons of undoubted ability who produce flashes of prophetic vision blurred by sometimes dangerous excesses. It is a fact of life that the future belongs to the young. But with their impatience, and their intolerance of ambiguity, young Catholics have in great part given up on the Church. Whether or not they will one day return will depend on the success which our many dedicated dissenters achieve in re-establishing the credibility of the Roman Catholic Church as a sign of redemptive love.

Thus, in summary, dissent in the U.S. Church has been ambiguous. An authoritarian style still characterizes the discourse and attitudes of most bishops. Yet, on the whole, the existence of public dissent has expressed and reinforced a new feeling of freedom. If ultimatums and anathemas can be avoided a bit longer, conscientious dissent might be converted here from a despairing cry of the young into a call to constructive action.

V. A New Community

Most problems of the American Church reflect the legalizing tendency of Catholic America's immigrant and defensive past. The hierarchical Church is a protective and reassuring structure. But the Church has to be more than that. As a community of the saved, its focus cannot be upon its administrative accomplishments nor exclusively upon cultural continuity with the past. The tradition of apostolic faith demands preaching a gospel which promises the disappearance of legal formalism in the End Time when communion will replace administration. Many dissenters believe that guarding *that* perspective would open the road to honest and genuine renewal in the American Church.

Gustavo Gutierrez

Contestation in Latin America

BY "contestation" I mean the act of opposing something as a
witness—a witness to a truth and/or a reality that constitutes the
source from which the act of opposing springs. So it is a total
attitude rooted in deep convictions, an attitude to life that shows
up primarily in action. But it is not only an act of witness: conflict
is inherent in it too. The witness is given in opposition .

This article forms part of a wider study of conflict in the
Church, and studies it within the Church in Latin America. But
a correct understanding of this attitude in Latin America immediately shows it to be rooted in *opposition to the established order*
in this continent of poverty and exploitation. And the Church is
not only tied to this established order in a thousand ways, conscious or unconscious, but is still, in a way, an integral part of it.
The Church legitimizes it, sacralizing situations of injustice and
oppression, or, at best, giving its blessing to superficial and ultimately fallacious efforts at reform and modernization. And in
many countries of the continent, four centuries of history have
produced a strong identification of Church structures with those
of the ruling social system.

Under these conditions, opposing the situation that obtains in
Latin America is to question the structures of the Church, and to
do so urgently and radically. For many, this also involves a basic
questioning of the mission of the Church. This is why all desire
for change in the Church springs from a will for revolutionary
social change, one that will break the present order of injustice
and alienation and begin to build a new society. This is because

the present situation of poverty and oppression is the greatest rejection of the gift of the Kingdom.

It is only in this context that the phenomenon of contestation in Latin America can be understood. This is what typifies it and distinguishes it from the forms it might take in other hemispheres. It is not a somewhat narcissistic internal Church affair, a result of the distance between the Church and the world that Vatican II did not really succeed in bridging. *Gaudium et Spes* talks of the Church in a world that is coming of age, and describes it in a way designed to reduce tensions and smooth down rough edges. But in Latin America (only?), the Church not merely *finds itself in*, but actively *forms part of*, a world in the throes of revolution, in which conflict and violence take on new forms every day. There is no disguising the fact that this is the case.

Growing minorities of Christians now realize this fact and take up positions, expressed in words and deeds, that are beginning to give the Church a new look. Many people are finding new hopes and new energies: the Church is changing. But not everyone agrees with them. And there are others who, seeing the weight of resistance to be overcome before the changes they seek can be brought about, and the incoherence and sometimes contradictions of the words and deeds of the reformers, remain, despite every-thing, indifferent to what is going on. There are also those who fear that the new efforts may somehow only serve to perpetuate the present state of affairs. With hopes and limitations, noble endeavours and open or marked resistance to them, optimism and pessimism, the present state of Latin America is full of ambiva-lence. Soon this ambivalence must be cleared away.

In the light of the foregoing attempt to define the essential lines of contestation in the Church in Latin America, we can now describe some of its main characteristics. This must be general, as there is no space for some aspects, nor for particularities affecting certain parts only. This is the price one has to pay for trying to give a brief account of a situation that is not only complex, but fluid.

I. A New Political Consciousness

The people of Latin America have lived for a long time in ignorance of the realities of their own situation. Such ignorance applied still more to the underlying causes of the situation. Then they suffered from the obfuscations of "objective studies" made by and for those outside countries and economic groups that had interests in the subcontinent. But, over the last few years, an approach has appeared, and is gaining momentum, that goes beyond the mere accumulation of statistics of illiteracy, infantile mortality, etc., which only served as an attempt to move the hearts of the rich nations to pity and benevolent aid. This was begging, when what was needed was a clear indication of an age-old injustice and a claiming of rights.

This approach, which attempts to go to the roots of the present situation, views the condition of Latin America in relation to the development and expansion of the rich capitalist nations. This condition then shows up, as an overall social fact, in its true light: a sub-product of the development of other nations. The dynamism of capitalist economy creates a centre and a periphery, producing at once progress and increasing riches for the few, and social unrest, political tension and poverty for the rest.

So Latin America comes to be seen in a *dependent* situation, in which the basic decisions are taken outside the subcontinent. This view is now taken by broad sectors of the Christian community as an accurate one of the social entity of which they form part. The Medellín Conference spoke of the state of "neo-colonialism" in which the peoples of Latin America live.[1] This interpretation of the state of affairs in terms of dependence on outside, connived at by the dominant groups in each country, is considered valid, "since it enables us to seek a causal explanation, to denounce tyranny, and to fight for an option for liberation that will lead us to a new society".[2]

Seeing things in this way presupposes a new and more mature political consciousness. For large sectors of the Latin American populace, this is the springboard to action. And so it is for those Christians who take a critical attitude to Church structures that are at once the product and the support of this state of dependence.

[1] Cf. the document, "Peace", produced by the Second General Conference of the Latin-American Episcopate, held in Bogotá in 1968 (henceforward referred to as *Medellín*).

[2] NADOC Latin-American documentation service, published in Lima, No. 147, on "Guidelines for the Andean regional meeting of Justice and Peace", p. 2.

This new political consciousness has left aside any sort of fatalistic approach to the present state of poverty and alienation, and has also abandoned any hope of being able to work progressively and gently towards a new form of society. The urgency of the task is all too clearly seen. So are the conflicts inherent in it.

II. The Option for Liberation

"Liberation" is a term that in the last few years has come to sum up the aspirations of the people of Latin America. It is a result of the new political consciousness I have described. Liberation means shaking off the yoke of economic, social, political and cultural domination to which we have been submitted. The view of development as a gradual process by which the underdeveloped countries overcome the obstacles that spring from their traditional social structures, and progress towards "modern society", or "industrial society", belongs to another kind of analysis of reality. This would have the underdeveloped countries be backward peoples, living at an "earlier" stage than the developed countries, and so having to repeat, more or less, the historical experiences of the latter on their journey to a mass-consumption society. It supposes a continuum between underdevelopment and development, and that underdeveloped and backward societies simply exist alongside developed, modern ones. But this, as we have seen, is just not the fact of the matter.

The term "liberation" is expressive of the conflict inherent in the situation. Development can only come to have meaning within a process of liberation that will break the present imbalance of the world economy and shatter the relationship of dependence it entails. Although it is closely related to this process, liberation means something still more. To be liberated is to take up the reins of one's own destiny, to be the architect of one's own history. This essential quality explains the strength of the movement in Latin America.

The Medellín Conference brought the term into contemporary ecclesial terminology. Despite current efforts to belittle the significance of this fact, the term and what it stands for have become the rallying point of the more alert Christian groups of the subcontinent. More important, the numbers of those Christians who desire to devote all their energies to furthering this process of liberation is growing all the time. This option for liberation on the part of a people long oppressed, alienated and plundered is coming to be the basic criterion for discerning real and up-to-date fidelity to the Gospel. It is also the horizon beckoning Latin-American Christians out of their narrowly ecclesiastical pre-occupations towards the wider perspective of throwing in their lot with a world in revolutionary ferment.[3]

Christians who oppose the present state of affairs in Latin America and seek to participate in the process of liberation are more and more openly taking the road of socialism. This social-ism, so the Argentinian priests of the Third World movement affirm, will be "a Latin-American socialism that will promote the advent of the New Man".[4] Linked to this goes a demand for common ownership of the benefits of production.[5] This demand runs counter to one of the pillars of present-day Latin-American society, the right to private property, to which the Church has lent, and still lends, its most explicit support, limiting itself at best to asking that private property should have a "social use". On the other hand, the rather special case of Cuba has now been followed by the example of Chile, in which the Church will have to learn to live—in the Latin-American context—with a society moving towards socialism.[6] This experience will undoubtedly have important consequences for those Christians who, with

[3] Cf. e.g., "Latin America, Continent of violence", a letter addressed to the Medellín Conference by more than a thousand priests, in *Signos de Renovación* (Lima, 1969), p. 105; "The second meeting of the priests' group of Golconda (Colombia)", in *ibid.*, p. 108; "Conclusions of the second national meeting of the priests' movement ONIS (Peru)", in *ONIS Declaraciones* (Lima, 1970), p. 29; "Letter of 120 Bolivian priests to their Episcopal Conference", in *NADOC* 148 (1970), p. 2.

[4] "Coincidencias básicas", in *Sacerdotes para el Tercer Mundo* (Buenos Aires, 1970), p. 69. Cf. also, "The second . . . Golconda meeting", in *Signos*, *op. cit.*, p. 12. ISAL Bolivia has the same commitment, expressed in *NADOC* 147 (1970), p. 6. Some bishops have also expressed the same views, such as Mgr Sergio Méndez (Cuernavaca, Mexico), in his Seventh Pastoral Letter of 1970 (Sept.), p. 4; Mgr Gerardo Valencia (Buenaventura, Colombia), in *CENCOS* (Mexico) of 10 Feb. 1970.

[5] "Private property and the new society" (declaration of ONIS), in the daily *Expreso* (Lima), 17 Aug. 1970; "Coincidencias . . .", in *op. cit.*, p. 70.

[6] First reactions are already appearing, such as the interesting analysis of the work of the University chaplains of Santiago, in *NADOC* 187 (1970).

others of other creeds, are struggling for the construction of a new society.

III. THE AFFIRMATION OF A CHARACTER OF ONE'S OWN

Aspiration to liberation from the present state of dependence, to control one's own destiny, brings another requirement for the Christian community: to affirm a character of its own. This requirement is another of the general characteristics of the phenomenon of contestation in this subcontinent.

The Church in Latin America was born alienated. It has not, from the start and despite some valiant efforts to the contrary, been the master of its own destiny. Decisions were taken outside the subcontinent. After the wars of independence of the last century, a sort of ecclesiastical "colonial treaty" was established. Latin America was to supply the "raw materials": the faithful, the Marian cult and popular devotions; Rome and the Churches of the Northern hemisphere were to supply the "manufactured goods": studies of Latin-American affairs, pastoral directives, clerical education, the right to name bishops—and even supply them—money for works and missions. In other words, the general dependent situation of Latin America is just as real in Church affairs.

With its centre outside the subcontinent, the Church in Latin America has turned its back on the process of liberation that germinated among the masses of the people. Faced with the growing involvement of so many Christians in this process, the Christian community is now going to have to take its fate into its own hands.

Only a Church that expresses the feelings of a people that has till now had no voice, that is now trying to realize what it is, can renew its fidelity to the Gospel, and in the process enrich the universal Church. This is why one of the main tasks for the Christian community in Latin America is to grow out of the colonial mentality.[7] The Medellín Conference was a first step on this road, the beginning—perhaps—of the process of the Latin-American Church affirming a character of its own.

[7] Cf. the Declaration of Itapoan (the department for social action of CELAM), in *Signos* . . . , p. 40; Working document of the second conference of Latin-American bishops, in *ibid.*, p. 215.

IV. EDUCATIVE EVANGELIZATION

If a situation of injustice and exploitation is incompatible with the Kingdom of God, the Word that announces the coming of the Kingdom must denounce this incompatibility. What this means is that those who hear the Word should, through the very act of listening to it, realize that they are oppressed and feel an impulse to pursue their own liberation. This educative dimension of the preaching of the Gospel, enemy of any aseptic presentation of the message, should lead to a basic revision of the pastoral practice of the Church in Latin America. This is what many Christian groups are asking, and beginning to practise; the urgency of the process of liberation and the need for the people to participate in it determine, for them, "that the first need is for an educative evangelization, one that frees, humanizes and advances mankind".[8]

Among other things, this would mean that the message has to be addressed to the most oppressed of the oppressed nations, and not to those who turn the injustices of the system to their own benefit. The message has to be carried in this way by a Church that now possesses a strong but ambiguous influence in Latin-American society. In this subcontinent we are a long way from the sort of secularization that has taken hold in the advanced industrial nations. But this is not to say that we are living in an earlier age and that progress will lead us inevitably to follow in their footsteps. We are rather living a process of secularization that might be called "unequal and combined". We are going through an original process that cannot be spelt out in simple terms, nor extrapolated from, made up of its own rhythm, co-existence with other forms of religious experience, other ways of working out the place of religion in the world, the possibility of being able to activate the potential of the Gospel, and of the Church, so as to contribute to the liberation of the people of Latin America. Here the Church is not simply a "private"

[8] "Document of the Pastoral Assembly of the Diocese of Salto", in *Iglesia Latinoamericana* (Uruguay, 1968), p. 373; cf. also *Juventud y Cristianismo* (conclusion reached by a seminar organized by CELAM's department of education) (Bogotá, 1969), p. 35; also "Gospel and subversion", the manifesto of twenty-one priests in Buenos Aires, in *Iglesia Latinoamericana*, p. 106; "Guidelines . . .", *op. cit.*, in *NADOC* 147, p. 4.

institution; its public nature makes its presentation of its message a public matter as well, without any effort on its part.

This social influence can and should be brought to bear in the direction of a rapid and thoroughgoing transformation of social structures in Latin America. There are those who fear that the Church will simply move from a position of compromise with the present order to one of compromise with the next, even if it is a more just one. There is some basis for this fear, and one must be careful. But the social influence of the Church is such a solid fact that not to use it in favour of the oppressed is to use it against them, and it is difficult to limit the effects of any change in advance. To remain silent is to become a different sort of "silent Church": one of silence in the face of the plunder and exploitation of the weak by the strong. And one can ask whether the best way for the Church to cut its ties with the present order—losing its ambiguous social prestige in the process—is not precisely to denounce the basic injustice on which it is based. There are many occasions when the Church is the only body in a position to raise its voice in protest, yet when it does so, it naturally makes an enemy of the ruling groups and becomes subject to political repression.[9]

In order to understand what the Church in Latin America must do now, and take action accordingly, one has to take account of its historical and social co-ordinates, its here and now. Otherwise we are left with an abstract and a-historical theology and commitment; or perhaps just a theology and an approach more careful of avoiding a repetition of past errors than of seeing the originality of the present situation and planning tomorrow accordingly. Such a course may be polemical, but it is one that many Christian groups put forward and have begun to put into practice.

The institutional position of the Church in the Latin-American situation is undoubtedly what lies behind the fact that its priests

[9] César Aguilar talks of the possibility of a new sort of "Underground Church" in Latin America: underground in relation to the political authorities, but not to the ecclesiastical authorities as it is in the rich countries: "Tendences et courants actuels du catholicisme latinoaméricain", in *IDOC-International* 30, p. 18; cf. also H. Borrat, *La Croix au sud* (Paris, 1970).

and religious at present constitute one of its most dynamic sectors. The last few years have seen the growth of groups of priests, both secular and religious, in several countries, coming together to channel and strengthen their growing desire to throw in their lot with the poor and the oppressed.[10] These groups seek to take an active part in the process of liberation, either through making political pronouncements or through practical involvement. The political impact of their efforts is clear; there have been many instances of friction between them and bishops and nuncios. creating difficult, conflict-laden situations. More importantly, it has also led to direct confrontations with the political authorities. It is common today for priests—and religious—to be regarded as "subversive" elements. Many are watched or wanted by the police; others are imprisoned, tortured, expatriated (Brazil, Bolivia, Colombia, the Dominican Republic, can all offer significant examples), or assassinated by terrorist anti-communist gangs.[11]

Stressing the part played by priests and religious is not to attribute any pre-eminence to them in the critical opposition to the *status quo* making itself felt in Christian circles. The laity were the first to tread this path. For the younger ones, the commitment is becoming more and more radical, but, for understandable reasons of efficacy, more and more exclusively political. Also, the average Latin-American Christian is going to be much less affected by the commitment of sections of the laity than by that of those more closely tied to the "institutional" aspects of the Church: religious, priests, bishops. This is why "priestly subversion" provokes such strong reactions: it contains the element of surprise for the defenders of the present situation. They are not used to it.[12]

Some bishops, scattered throughout the subcontinent, support

[10] "Priests for the Third World" of Argentina, and the "Priests' movement ONIS" of Peru, are perhaps the most organized and active. The Golconda group in Colombia was until recently, and has left a deep impression. There are similar groups in Ecuador, Chile, and Guatemala, and other kinds of organization in Bolivia and other countries.

[11] Such as the case of Henrique Pereira Neto, a priest in Recife, Brazil.

[12] *Apropos* of this situation Fidel Castro has said: "These are the paradoxes of history. When we see sections of the clergy becoming revolutionary forces, how are we to resign ourselves to seeing sectors of Marxism in the forces of the Church?" (Closing address to the Congress of Intellectuals, 12 Jan. 1968, in F. Castro, *Revolution cubaine* (Paris, 1969), II, p. 253.

these attitudes of "subversion". These are generally isolated individuals, but in one or two cases, whole hierarchies are in favour.[13] For the bishops, the most usual vehicle of protest is the written word, but there have been cases where their publications have been accompanied by physical acts. Fear of this sort of approach is growing among the bishops as a whole, but then so is the frequency of deciding on it. On this plane, too, we are approaching a resolution that, as usual, will leave the undecided by the wayside, but it will certainly not be the over-simplified outcome expected by those who see all the troubles of the Church in Latin America in the form of direct opposition between the rulers and the ruled in the Church. The reason for this I have already stressed several times: here, internal opposition in the Church is only part of a wider opposition to an unjust order of which the Church itself is a part.

V. Solidarity in Poverty

One of the most insistent requests from many sections of the Christian community is that the Church in Latin America should give a witness of poverty. This is a really essential proof of its authenticity. Everything it does and says about the poverty and injustice rife in the subcontinent will remain empty deeds and words unless it is backed up by a real shedding of the Church's own riches, and a real identification with the poor. Let us make no mistake about this: the overall image of the Church is not exactly that of a poor Church. The final communiqué of Medellín recognizes this with honesty, and with sadness. In fact one could say that signs to the contrary are legion. But it should be stressed that the sort of witness of poverty needed has to be at once *a solidarity with the poor and a protest against the poverty* in which they live.[14]

[13] There was the famous case of the excommunication of three senior officials of the Paraguayan government by the national heirarchy. This is a weapon little used today, but what is even more unusual in this case is that it was done in defiance of the ruling clique, which claimed to be defending "the values of Western, Christian civilization": see "The October events in Asunción", in *Spes* (Montevideo), 3 (Nov. 1969), pp. 6–9.

[14] Cf. *Medellín*, documents produced by the bishops of Uruguay, Bolivia, Peru and Mexico.

Poverty in this sense is an act of love for the poor and a commitment to freeing them from the situation in which they exist. It has a redemptive value. If egoism is the ultimate cause of man's exploitation and alienation, love for the poor is the basic reason for voluntary poverty. Christian poverty is meaningless unless it is a commitment to solidarity with the poor, with those who suffer hunger and injustice, in order to bear witness to the evil that this hunger and injustice represent. Therefore one is not seeking a romantic idealization of poverty, but a recognition of it as the evil it is, in order to protest against it and struggle for its abolition.

Inasmuch as this solidarity and poverty have a liberating significance, so, in the Latin-American situation, they obviously and inevitably have a political significance. The "poor" today are the oppressed, those despoiled by the powerful, the proletariat fighting for the most elementary rights, the exploited peasant class, the country fighting for its freedom. So becoming poor in Latin America means taking the side of the oppressed against the oppressors.

There are broad sections of the Christian community now thinking along these lines, initiating experiments and presenting demands to the Church authorities.[15]

VI. New Church Structures

All the requirements I have outlined so far: for a prophetic opposition, the affirmation of a character of one's own, an educative evangelization of the oppressed and a witness of poverty, all point to the fact that the present structures of the Church no longer correspond to present needs. They seem outdated and lacking in the dynamism needed to face the serious new questions facing the Church. As a group of Bolivian priests has declared: "The very structure of which we form part often prevents us from acting in a true spirit of evangelism".[16]

There is a particular need for a change of style in the priest's

[15] Cf. e.g., the letter from eighty Bolivian priests in *Signos* ..., p. 161; the 1967 Declaration of 300 Brazilian priests, in *ibid.*, pp. 154–5; the conclusions of the first week of overall pastoral activity in El Salvador, June 1970, in *NADOC* 174; "Poverty and the religious life in Latin America", the Report of the Latin-American Conference of Religious, CLAR (Bogotá, 1970).

[16] The letter from eighty Bolivian priests, in *Signos* ..., p. 160.

life, especially as regards his commitment to the creation of a new society. Many priests and religious are beginning to tire of the weight of resistance they have to overcome within the Church, and to be disillusioned by the ineffectiveness of work that they consider purely "religious", with little contact with the daily reality of the life of the people. This leads them to reformulate the present form of the priestly ministry or the religious life, and sometimes even the very meaning of priesthood or religious profession in the commitment to the oppressed and their fight for freedom. This is the reason why questions that elsewhere seem so important in relation to the religious or priestly life are somewhat pushed into the background in Latin America.[17]

VII. A New Kind of Ecumenism

The present situation in Latin America is leading to increasing contact between Christians of different denominations but sharing the same political commitment. This favours the formation of ecumenical groups in which Christians put their common faith at the service of the creation of a more just society. An example of this is the ISAL (Church and Society for Latin America) movement, which is an important exercise in collaboration between Christians of different denominations within the framework of a clear commitment to political liberation. Their common struggle makes the traditional subject-matter of ecumenism seem outdated, and they are following new courses in the quest for unity.

With such a commitment, in fact, the axis of "division" among Christians shifts: the relevant differences are in the stances adopted towards the existing social order. There are Christians among those who benefit from and defend the existing social order, and among its victims and those who are struggling to change it.

[17] Jorge Vernazza, in the name of the Permanent Secretariat of Priests for the Third World, wrote to the *Echanges et Dialogue* movement of France: "And it is the Church that should announce and promote this liberation ... it is the Church that we believe to have an enormous educative potential with the people.... We believe that numerous sociological and historical signs point to the fact that our clerical state in Latin America should be lived in a form different to yours.... This is why it seems to us that it is our very commitment to man and to the cause of revolution that forces us to remain clergymen" (Letter 10 Dec. 1969, in *ENLACE*—the bulletin of the Priests for the Third World movement—10, Buenos Aires, 1970, p. 23).

There are Christian oppressors and Christian oppressed. Under these conditions unity among Christians depends on a totally new set of factors: the unity still to be sought is within each confessional Church with regard to a social and economic framework whose true nature can no longer be hidden.[18] This shift of focus on the unity question leads to new courses of action, and among those taking these courses will be the minority opposition groups of the different Christian confessions.

Where will all these efforts lead? It is hard to say, and it should not be forgotten that they are minority activities, leaving the bulk of the Latin-American Christian community untouched. The influence of these minorities is growing, but they still lack the strength to back up their objectives, at least as long as they are trying to widen their basis of support and not decline into élitist groups. They are still minorities with tasks to perform, rather than with achievements behind them.

All the signs point, none the less, to the fact that we are moving towards modes of Church presence—and structures—whose radical novelty cannot be mapped out on the basis of today's experience. What is clear is that this will never come about without a recognition of the fact that the Gospel is necessarily in opposition to this society of injustice and plunder—which means a realization that the meaning of the Gospel is not to be watered down. This is also a way of affirming the primacy of the Lord in our lives, of bearing concrete witness to the love of God through active service to the people of this subcontinent. Changes in the Church will be made because of this. To look for changes for their own sake would be to seek the survival of the Church. And this is not the question. The Church's task is to serve, not to survive. The rest will be added to it.

[18] On the subject of the Evangelical churches, Ch. Lalive D'Epinay writes: "Between these two forms of the Church there is a qualitative divide which makes any reformist change impossible. The transformation of Protestantism in Latin America will involve radical opposition to the first form, it means breaching the walls of that petrified structure so as to bring it tumbling down . . . radical opposition alone can lead to new ways being opened": "La Iglesia evangélica y la revolución latinoamericana", in *CIDOC* (Curenavaca), 78 (Dec. 1968), p. 12.

Translated by Paul Burns

Hans van Pinxteren

Contestation in Africa

IN THIS article, I shall confine myself to the African Catholic churches south of the Sahara, in which "contestation is not current".[1] In the first section, I will try to explain this statement by discussing a number of factors in the past and the present which show that Africa is in a very special position with regard to the phenomenon of contestation. In the second part, I will examine the extent to which contestation in fact occurs there.

I. REASONS FOR THE RELATIVE ABSENCE OF CONTESTATION

The African churches were the product of—and are still characterized by—nineteenth- and twentieth-century missionary activities, which took place during the period of Western colonialism in which submissiveness was expected and encouraged. Missionary work became a well-organized movement conducted by foreign institutions under the central authority of the Congregation for the Propagation of the Faith. One of the results of this situation was—and still is—a certain passivity. The Africans themselves are not expected to take the initiative,[2] but to receive. It is therefore not surprising that many of them have the attitude of beggars. Missionary work has in general been characterized by great activity along familiar lines, and by very

[1] P. Wanko, "Paul VI en Afrique", *Église Vivante* 21 (1969), p. 444.
[2] "For long enough our problems have been solved for us, without us and even in spite of us", *Des prêtres noirs s'interrogent* (Rencontres 47) (Paris, ²1957), p. 16. This publication is the first and almost the only expression of contestation on the part of Africans.

little critical reflection. The churches are above all concerned with education, health and development plans.

There is, in this situation, very little scope for contestation, which arises from firm personal conviction. For many Africans, however, becoming or being a Christian was—and again, still is —less a question of deep personal commitment and more a question of joining a Church which offers the possibility of social improvement, a choice frequently determined by chance circumstances. The "easy" African mission has hardly ever been marked by great religious depth, and this perhaps explains the indifference in Africa towards renewal in the Church.

There are also very few effective means of communication by which the spirit of contestation can be disseminated in Africa. The Church newspapers and bulletins are to some extent subject to "control"—they give the impression that everything in the African garden is lovely. The size of the continent, the number of languages and national boundaries also mean that contestation has little chance of success. It is, in a word, very difficult to obtain clear and precise information about this subject. The only real source would seem to be the readers' letters in the national newspapers.[3]

Are the Africans contestation-minded? I think it may be true to say that, for Africans as well as "for the majority of Asiatics, there is a basic need of harmony, tolerance, unity and peace. We, on the other hand, ... need to differentiate and to dispute."[4] It is also true that contestation flourishes in an atmosphere of individualism, and the traditional tribal structure of African society militates against individual opposition, which is seen as a social vice.

Yet any conclusion that there is little or no contestation in Africa may be challenged by the successful political contestation of the colonial system throughout the continent. Politically, however, the Africans have long been deeply and personally involved, whereas they have never been equally committed Church members. Moreover, it cannot be denied that political contestation has always been the concern of the few. The great mass of the people

[3] This should be a fruitful field for research into contestation in Africa.
[4] A.-M. H(enry), "Le poids de l'Occident, compte rendu du colloque", in *Parole et Mission* 13 (1970), p. 489.

are passive, the means of communication are poor, and political movements have always received support from outside Africa.

Another question which we are bound to ask is whether the African movement of "independent churches" can be interpreted as a phenomenon of contestation. This movement, which is quite unique in its extent in Africa,[5] is usually discussed under the heading of schism, division or sectarianism. Purely religious and ecclesiological factors are not the only elements in this movement, which is, in any case, not directly related to the phenomenon of contestation, mainly because it is seldom the aim of the "independent churches" to change or reform the "mother Church". There is simply a spontaneous emergence of a new church or a movement away from the original Church, without any conscious opposition—very much like the emergence of a new clan within the existing tribe.

This formation of new, independent churches may express dissatisfaction with the established Church order, but there is no direct contestation, although it may well serve as an indirect contestation, so long as the original churches regard the phenomenon as an implicit criticism of their complexity, unsuitability or alien character.

If Africans, and especially individual Africans, are reluctant to express direct contestation within the churches, this is certainly not the case with the foreign missionaries in Africa. These men and women are directly involved in the problems confronting the African churches and are personally affected by the constant crisis in the missions, caused by shortage of money and workers. Above all, they want to correct the mistakes made by their predecessors in the mission field and to build up an authentic and living African Christian community. In their attempts to do this, they must often directly contest the existing Church order, most of the undesirable elements of which are to be found everywhere in the world. In their contestation, however, the African missionaries tend to stress the Western and un-African character of certain Church structures, attitudes and traditions.

[5] Out of many books and articles on this subject, I would select D. B. Barrett, *Schism and Renewal in Africa. An Analysis of Six Thousand Contemporary Religious Movements* (Nairobi, 1968).

II. Signs of Contestation in Africa

Although the foreign missionaries are more ready than the Africans to contest Church structures, this contestation is less acceptable in the present stage of development of the African churches precisely because they are foreigners. The churches are at the moment no longer dependent missions, but not yet fully independent churches. Their opposition to the earlier, missionary situation is the first sign of an awakening self-consciousness and of a movement towards independence. When the foreign missionaries on whom they have for so long been dependent question the existing Church structure in Africa, the Africans themselves, perhaps confused by this attitude on the part of those who introduced that structure into their continent, often respond by perpetuating it.

This is why the African Church leaders have been so vigorous in rejecting the phenomenon of contestation, especially as pursued by the foreign missionaries and their African followers. In July 1969, Cardinal Zoungrana of Upper Volta made a statement at the first Symposium of Episcopal Conferences in Africa and Madagascar, which has since become a watchword throughout the whole of Africa: "Let us say clearly, our very being must not be conferred upon us from outside."[6] He repeated this at the second Symposium in August 1970, where he also spoke about the "scandal of contestation",[7] a subject which also had wide repercussions. Archbishop Gantin of Dahomey quoted the Cardinal's statement and went on: "Maybe in other continents, the words 'submission' and 'dependence' are unwelcome to the ears of those who want contestation at all costs. Here we are in Africa, not in Holland or France...."[8] In his speech welcoming Pope Paul VI to Uganda, Cardinal Rugambwa of Tanzania said: "The present state of contestation in the bosom of the Church appears to us to go beyond the bounds of dialogue and research."[9] The same cardinal said elsewhere: "We must remember the Church in Africa is not the Church of Europe or the Church of the United States.... Our problems are not exactly the same as theirs.... I

---

[6] *Symposium Dossier* (Gaba-Kampala, 1969), p. 17.
[7] *Uganda Catholic Information News Bulletin (UCI)*, 28.8.1970, p. 5.
[8] *UCI*, 31.10.1969, p. 4.   [9] *Symposium Dossier*, p. 47.

believe that the initiative for change and adaptation for the Church in Africa should come from Africans."[10] Mgr Ntuyahaga of Burundi called Europe "contagious",[11] and Mgr Yungu of Congo-Kinshasa remarked: "The Church in Europe has its own problems. Yesterday it was dialogue; today it is contestation. . . . We are frightened by the reaction that this contestation may arouse [in the young churches]."[12]

The African bishops have also objected to radical theological, liturgical and pastoral renewal and to criticism of the structures of the Church, of papal authority, of priestly celibacy and of the papal teaching on birth control.[13] Refresher courses in Europe have to a great extent been replaced by local courses. There has been opposition to "importing the phenomenon of contestation"[14] and to the idea that Europe can continue to help Africa as a mission not of domination, but of encounter.[15]

There can be no doubt, then, that there are signs of contestation even among the Africans themselves and I should like to conclude by reviewing some of these briefly under eight main subject headings.

1. Doubts are often expressed about obligatory priestly celibacy,[16] usually within the whole context of the priestly ministry[17]

---

[10] *UCI*, 14.8.1970, p. 4.   [11] *Au Cœur de l'Afrique* 10 (1970), p. 97.

[12] "What a Congolese Bishop Thinks of Contestation; Its Consequences in Africa", in *Christ to the World* 15 (1970), pp. 397–8.

[13] *Christian to the World* 15 (1970), pp. 394–6; *UCI, passim; Parole et Mission* 13 (1970), pp. 485–504; *Église Vivante* 21 (1969), pp. 439–40; *African Ecclesiastical Review (AFER)* 12 (1970), pp. 363–6; *Sharing* (Gaba), August 1970, pp. 10–11; E. Klausener, *Steht der Papst gegen die Kirche? Afrikas Bischöfe fragen: werden Europas Katholiken dekadent?* (Berlin, 1970); see also the report in *UCI*, 20.11.1970, p. 5, of the urgent request made by President Banda of Malawi to the bishops to be on their guard against "progressive religious ideas" and of his warning, "The modern trend in European countries is to question everything, even the existence of God. I shall not tolerate that my people become confused." See also *Sharing*, December 1970, p. 2.

[14] *AFER* 12 (1970), pp. 234–43; *Église Vivante* 22 (1970), pp. 379–80 481–2; *Au Cœur de l'Afrique* 10 (1970), pp. 97–8; *Sharing*, November–December 1969, p. 10; November 1970, pp. 5–6.

[15] *Parole et Mission* 13 (1970), p. 500.

[16] See, for example, the recent numbers of *AFER*.

[17] See, for example, the report of the secretariat of the Pastoral and Research Institute of Tanzania, Bukumbi, in the *Seminar Study Year (SSY)*, 1969.

and of the difficulty of dealing with the shortage of priests in the traditional ways.[18] The function of the minor seminaries[19] and the current forms of training for the priesthood are also criticized in this context.[20] There are also objections to the fact that these problems are not open for public discussion and research.[21]

2. There is contestation about the way in which the bishops exercise their authority, the absence of dialogue between them and priests and laypeople, and the very slow setting up of the structures for this dialogue (pastoral councils and so on) recommended by the Second Vatican Council.[22]

3. In the liturgy, conservatism on Africa[23] and the European, even Roman, character of the new instructions are criticized.[24]

4. Every obstacle to the development of a truly indigenous Church is contested—on the one hand, the imposition of Western parochial structures, teaching about marriage and catechetics and, on the other, the neglect of the traditionally African religious life, and the dependence of the African churches on the missionary institutions.[25]

5. The European historical background to ecumenism is not accepted by the Africans, who are looking for distinctively African ways to reunion.[26]

[18] *Ibid.*; *Service* (Bukumbi), 1970, No. 8, pp. 1-20; No. 4, pp. 8-15; *Sharing*, November–December 1969, p. 10; March 1970, pp. 8-10.

[19] *AFER* 10 (1968), pp. 405-9; 12 (1970), pp. 327-34.

[20] *AFER* 12 (1970), pp. 228-33.

[21] *Service*, 1970, No. 8, p. 7; *Sharing*, December 1970, p. 3.

[22] Report of a survey among Congolese priests ("In the Congolese Church, contestation is not concerned with the essence of authority, its ontological structure, but with its exercise"); *SSY*, 1969, Tanzania; *Service*, 1970, No. 1, p. 13; *AFER* 10 (1968), pp. 123, 125-7.

[23] *AFER* 11 (1969), pp. 353-4.

[24] *Église Vivante* 22 (1970), p. 170; *Au Cœur de l'Afrique* 10 (1970), pp. 199-200.

[25] A great deal has been written about this question, especially in African journals. Of these, I would single out *Des prêtres noirs s'interrogent*, cf. n. 2; S. Hertlein, *Christentum und Mission im Urteil neoafrikanischen Prosaliteratur* (Münsterschwarzach, 1962); M. Hebga, *et al.. Afrika en Christendom* (Hilversum and Maaseik, 1967) (*Personnalité africaine et catholicisme*, Paris, 1963); Ram Desai, *Christianity in Africa as seen by the Africans* (Denver, 1962); G. Deroy, "Une critique africaine du christianisme occidental", in *Église Vivante* 19 (1967), pp. 40-50; B. Nkuissi, "Adaptation missionaire", in *Église Vivante* 19 (1967), pp. 351-61; *Christians in Ghanaian Life* (Seminar Lay Apostolate) (Accra, 1968).

[26] *Internationale Katholieke Informatie* 3 (1969), No. 19, pp. 23-4; *Parole*

6. "Romanism" in general or in its details—papal envoys, the Roman practice of secrecy and appointments, for example—is sharply contested.[27]

7. The attitude of Rome towards the Church-State relationship in Portuguese East Africa is also contested.[28]

8. Finally, another cause of contestation is the Church's attitude of aloofness towards the question of African nationalism.[29]

For reasons of space, I have not made any assessment of the relative frequency, the importance, or the legitimacy of these contestations. Two final comments would not be out of place. Firstly, it is mainly priests—and increasingly African priests—who are contesting. The lay people have not yet really "come of age" in Africa and their voices are scarcely heard in the Catholic press. The younger generation may, of course, change this situation. Secondly, there is another possible line of research which would be very fruitful both for the Catholic Church and for the other churches—an investigation of what has not—or not yet—been contested in the African churches.

---

et Mission 13 (1970), p. 487; see also *UCI*, 30.1.1970, p. 1: Professor J. S. Mbiti of Makerere is reported to have made "a plea . . . to the masses of Christians to disagree with their leaders if they blocked the way to a speedy unity of Christians" and to have made the suggestion "to abolish this Week of Prayer for Christian Unity . . . and to supersede it with the real thing: the organic unity of God's people in Christ"; see also *Sharing*, March 1970, p. 2.

[27] *Sharing*, March 1970, pp. 8–10; December 1970, pp. 2–3; *Service*, 1970, No. 4, p. 10; see also the report of the Congolese priests, n. 22.

[28] *Église Vivante* 21 (1969), pp. 272, 294–5; *Sharing*, May 1970, p. 11; November 1970, p. 4; *UCI*, 22.5.1970, pp. 2–3.

[29] *Pastoral Guide* (Uganda), October 1970, pp. 41–53; September 1970, pp. 18–24; *SSY*, 1969, Tanzania.

Translated by David Smith

Tissa Balasuriya

Contestation in the Church in Asia

CONTESTATION in the Church in modern Asia is a very recent phenomenon and manifests itself openly only in places where Catholics are fairly numerous and well rooted in their environment. Most Asian churches are very small in numbers, isolated from others, struggling to survive among a mass of believers of other religions or under Communism, ministered to largely by foreign missionaries, with a clergy formed in the pre-Vatican II theology, and bishops heavily dependent financially on Rome or their aiding agencies and intellectually fairly innocent of radical thinking.

However, after Vatican II there have been openings for dialogue and consultation through seminars, synods, commissions, pastoral councils, senates of priests, conferences of religious superiors, etc. These have created an atmosphere of expectation of change, and in some places have led to disappointment when changes were slow in forthcoming.

The traditional Asian mentality is generally one of passive obedience and respect for authority and does not make for contestation. There is however a growing contestation in certain countries like the Philippines, India, Ceylon, and less openly in some others. Each country has its peculiar situation, especially in the political sphere, and this influences the Church very much.

The areas of contestation relate to political options, social reform, style of life of clergy and bishops, use of Church resources, relationships within the Church, seminary formation, relations with Marxism, other religions, liturgical experimentation, clerical

60

celibacy and birth control. However, almost everywhere in Asia, except in the Philippines, the contestation exists more in thought and word than in action and open demonstration, and is more an affair of small private groups than public and widespread. Catholics are reluctant to criticize the Church in public because of their minority consciousness and past presentation of a monolithic front. Where Catholics are very few there is hardly any open contestation—even though some may be unhappy with the *status quo*. This is the position in Israel, Syria, Iraq, Iran, Arabia, Turkey, Jordan, Pakistan, Afghanistan, Nepal, Bhutan, Sikkim, North Borneo, Saba and Sarawak, Laos, Cambodia, Thailand and Macao. Hence in the whole of West Asia there is no contestation but rather a problem of survival.*

Another group of countries is dominated by the problem of Communism and the war of the past two decades. Thus China, Tibet, North and South Korea, North and South Vietnam, Taiwan, Hongkong, Macao, Laos, Cambodia, Thailand, Indonesia and even Malaysia and Singapore. In Communist-controlled areas there is no evidence of contestation in the Church. The fear of Communism and the refugee problem make Taiwan, Hongkong, South Vietnam and South Korea more orthodox and loyal to the Church in an anti-Communist stand. Contestation is seen as softness towards Communism, and is therefore largely unpopular.

In South Vietnam there is a sort of contestation by a relatively small group of priests, religious and lay leaders who want a more pacific approach towards the Viet Cong and North Vietnam. They demand the withdrawal of the U.S. forces and protest against Government cruelties to prisoners. Since these points are against the general line of policy of the Catholics this group is regarded as doubtful in its loyalty to the Church.

In Thailand, Malaysia and Singapore there is a gradual awakening among students, young intellectuals and their chaplains to the necessity for reforms in the Church and for Christians to take a greater interest in national affairs. Last year in Thailand they mildly recommended this to their Episcopal Council.

In Indonesia the Catholics were strongly anti-Communist,

* I have no information regarding Lebanon.

particularly because of the Communist coup in September 1965. Now there are groups that, under the influence of new ideas, advocate openness in their approach towards Marxism, Islam and Nationalism. They want to attack corruption and the social injustices in the country. This is a form of contestation against the Catholics, including some leading churchmen, who support the present regime and its strong anti-Communist line.

In Taiwan the Catholic leadership strongly opposes Chinese Communism. There is little evidence of any contestation of this position. Renewal within the Church is even delayed due to the fear of Communism. Only when the generation of adults who have suffered under Communism passes away can we expect more openness of Catholics towards these issues.

In Hongkong the situation is largely similar in so far as the population is Chinese. But the greater openness of Hongkong to the rest of the world has brought about quicker re-thinking among them, even with reference to Communism. In 1970, at the Convention of the Diocese of Hongkong, a suggestion was made that the Church in Hongkong should encourage a dialogue with Communism because Communists also wanted an equitable distribution of wealth and might one day control Hongkong. This caused such a furore at the Convention and in the Press that the bishop of the diocese stopped discussion of the topic; many regarded this as a veto on dialogue with Marxism. In Burma the problem of the Church is rather one of survival, due to the difficulties imposed by the present circumstances; hence there is hardly any question of contestation.

Japan has a very small Catholic community, in a highly developed society. There is no publicly displayed contestation of the European or American type, but there is a slowly rising moral pressure for greater participation in decision making, for representation at the parochial and diocesan levels of planning and command and, above all, for less structured friendly relationships between bishops and their priests. The younger priests question celibacy and birth control. Yet respect for authority is the main attitude of the Catholics in Japan. A goodly number of priests both foreign and Japanese have given up their ministry—and this may mean that, where contestation is unlikely to succeed, fading away from the scene is seen as a way out.

In India the Catholic groups are small isolated pockets in the Hindu-Moslem mass, except in certain areas like Goa, Kerala, Tamilnad, and cities such as Bombay, Calcutta and Bangalore. Hence in most of India there is no direct contestation as such. But there is a growing mental contestation, by the élite, of the prevailing sense of values and priorities. Within the dioceses, parishes, religious communities and institutions there is a certain measure of dialogue, but also a big gap between verbal acceptance of conclusions and their implementation; and this leads to much insecurity and frustration.

While contestation is still mental and verbal in most parts of India as in the rest of Asia, there have been some instances of active open contestation. This is prominent *in the political field* where Indian Catholics particularly in Kerala openly supported the Marxists, in spite of the views of the Hierarchy. This is a phenomenon that exists even from the period before Vatican II. Kerala, which has about half the Catholic population of India, is the state which voted for the world's first elected Marxist Government. A good number of young radicals leave the Church because they do not find among Christians an adequately far-reaching commitment. They are critical of the Hierarchy's support for the Congress Government—and now apparently with the Old Congress and the Right-wing groups. Some have joined the Naxalites, who are committed to violence.

There is sporadic contestation in regard to the liturgy—especially in seminaries and youth groups; but this is not yet a significant movement. In inter-religious relations there is a fairly broad tolerance of experiments in different styles of life, which are not contestation, even though they would be if they were carried out in less tolerant countries.

The All India Seminar (May 1969), after much discussion and hesitation, mildly recommended that Pope Paul rethink his decision about birth control in view of the enormous difficulties in India. Catholic students recently demonstrated in Kerala against a plan to put up four churches for four different denominations in the same compound. Yet they do not seem to have won the day.

Students who are more sensitive to social issues feel particularly alienated from the Church. This phenomenon has become increasingly clear at Pan Asian Conferences of Catholic students, as in Hongkong (July 1970). Consequently chaplains too are unable to mediate satisfactorily between students and the colleges or dioceses. Chaplains, and nuns too, tend towards mental or verbal contestation in the first instance. In the coming years contestation is likely to grow in the areas where Catholics are in bigger numbers.

Contestation in Ceylon goes back to the nationalization of the 750 Catholic schools in 1960. The Church authorities and most of the Catholics bitterly opposed the take-over of the schools. Yet some Catholics, including many teachers, supported it openly.

After Vatican II, several publications (e.g., *Forum, Quest, Outlook*) and the national Press discussed problems of the renewal of the Church. *Outlook* was founded by laymen because of censorship of Catholic publications. During the National Synod (1968), there was a strong demand for overall reforms in the Church. The Socio-religious Survey conducted by Canon François Houtart and his team from the University of Louvain also revealed how estranged the Church leadership was from the aspirations of the people.

As a result of the prolonged dispute in Chilaw diocese connected with the relationship between the bishop and the clergy and the appointment of a coadjutor bishop, an apostolic visitor was appointed by Rome to try to heal the rift that rather deeply divided the diocese. Quite a few priests have given up the ministry in recent years in the search for a more credible witness; some have opted for marriage. There has been an occasional contestation over the appointment of chaplains for lay movements.

Recently the seminarists in Kandy confronted the bishops with demands for changes in the style of life of seminarists, and in the content and methods of teaching. Many promising young seminarists have left in the course of the last few years. There is still no open demonstration of contestation in Ceylon.

It is in the Philippines that the greatest extent of contestation takes place in Asia. This is understandable because of the numbers of Catholics in the Philippines and the rather "established" nature of Catholicism there. During the past three or four years, especially since 1969, contestation has taken the form of open opposition to certain alleged malpractices in the Church. The contestation centres upon problems such as the wealth of some of the dioceses, the relations between the Hierarchy and the political powers, the treatment of priests in the different dioceses, the appointment of a bishop without consulting the clergy of the diocese, the role of Radio Veritas, freedom in the Church—including the right of honest dissent, celibacy, birth control, the clerical habit, the participation of the clergy in politics, the freedom of religious, the need for the Church to work for social justice, accounts of dioceses, disclosure of assets, and so on.

The main area of contestation has been the archdiocese of Manila. There the target of attack has been the Cardinal, whom contestants—including priests, religious and laity—have openly accused of being extremely rich and not using his power, wealth or influence for socially beneficial purposes or in a manner consonant with the Gospel. Last November they asked for his resignation in the presence of the Pope. Students demonstrated for these objectives. The Cardinal retaliated with charges of disobedience and of pro-Communist leanings in the contestants.

The Church in the Philippines is in a state of real ferment. The reform-minded priests have a forum in the Philippine Priests Inc., and in their publication, the *Philippine Priests' Forum*. Some Jesuit fathers in Manila have had acute disagreements with the Cardinal over these issues. Movements such as the Free Farmers have supported the priests, religious and students in this contestation. Contestation has had the effect of compelling ecclesiastical authorities to discuss matters with their priests, religious and laity—especially the students. These positive results strengthen the trend towards contestation, which has helped to strengthen the organizations of priests and students, and has awakened Catholics to a consciousness of their role and potentialities in bringing about reforms.

It would seem that contestation in the Church in the Philippines is only at its beginning; it might grow to something like the position in Latin America or the United States. In this sense, the Philippines are really exceptional in Asia; this indicates the type of situation which can heighten contestation in the Church. The Philippines are said to be ripe for a social revolution—because of the existing injustices, inequalities and corruption, and the growing exasperation of the people.

Maxwell Charlesworth

Contestation in Australia

COMPARED with the Church in Europe and the U.S.A., there are remarkably few tensions, creative or otherwise, within the Catholic Church in Australia. To a very large extent, the institutional structures of the Australian Church, the relationship between clergy and laity, and the theological and pastoral and social attitudes of Australian Catholics, have remained untouched by the revolution set in train by Vatican II. In the Australian Catholic community there is no real challenge to the authority of the bishops or of Rome; there have been no large-scale defections from the priesthood (though there has been a decline in vocations to the priesthood and the religious life); there is no "underground Church" of any importance; there has been no serious attempt to change the traditional institutions, and very little theological or social radicalism among Catholics. *Humanae Vitae* and all that it stood for was not contested by Australian Catholics in the way in which it was opposed by a significant number of American Catholics, and on his recent visit to Australia Pope Paul was enthusiastically welcomed by the Catholic community. There are, no doubt, hints and suggestions of strains and tensions within the Australian Church, but—relatively to Europe and the U.S.A.—contestation is not a significant and central issue in Australian Catholicism. Whether this relative peace and calm is a sign of health and something to be thankful for, or on the other hand it is a sign of inertia and paralysis, the Australian Church does enjoy a kind of pre-Vatican II peace and tranquillity at the present time.

The Catholic Church in Australia, like Australian society itself, is no more than a hundred and fifty years old, and in those few years it has grown from a group of some three hundred Irish and English convicts into a Church of 2·5 million members, representing almost a quarter of the total Australian population. The early clergy and bishops, after a succession of remarkable English priests, were solidly Irish, and the Irish influence remained dominant in Australian Catholicism until very recently. It would, perhaps, be more exact to speak of a Romano-Irish influence since, as a contemporary historian has pointed out (John N. Molony, *The Roman Mould of the Australian Catholic Church*, Melbourne, 1969), the Irish bishops who came to Australia were mostly products of Roman seminaries and cast very much in the conservative Roman mould. Irish-Australian Catholicism was responsible for very substantial achievements, but also for many of the limitations and inhibitions that still affect the Church in Australia. For example, there was until fairly recently a powerful strain of clericalism in the Australian Church and the laity were seen very much as second-class citizens. Even now, when there is a small but vocal lay intelligentsia (located largely in the state universities), the laity have little real power or influence within the Church, and they have almost no journals or other means of expression through which their voice could be heard. The monthly journal, the *Catholic Worker*, is the only independent lay Catholic organ of any significance. Recently, however, there have been associations of lay Catholics formed in order to promote critical discussion within the Church. Some of the lay intelligentsia speak pessimistically of a "crisis of confidence" in the Church, and of the Church in Australia "losing the educated classes" just as the nineteenth-century Church in Europe lost the working class. This tension between university-educated Catholics and the older clergy and bishops has not, however, been expressed in open conflict. Instead, an increasing number of younger Catholics tend to dismiss the institutional Church as being irrelevant to their concerns and interests. Their attitude is one of indifference rather than of contestation.

Some of the younger clergy have founded an independent national association of priests to press for reforms within the priesthood and the Church, and some of the diocesan "priests' senates" have taken up mildly critical attitudes. The Melbourne priests' senate, for example, recently questioned the Hierarchy's decision to hold an international eucharistic congress in Melbourne. It cannot be said, however, that these moves are very significant. The recent failure of the independent and "reformist" journal, *Priests' Forum*, is symptomatic in this respect.

The Irish background has also been responsible for what might be called the pragmatism of Australian Catholicism. In other words, Australian Catholics have for the most part been preoccupied with practical works—building churches, setting up various social services, maintaining a comprehensive Catholic primary and secondary school system—and there has been very little interest in theological speculation. The Australian Church has not given birth to any theological innovators or pace-setters, such as Professor Hans Küng, to challenge traditional ideas—let alone any radical theologians of the American or Dutch kind.

Australian Catholics have always been in a minority, and tended to feel in the past that they were a ghetto within the larger Protestant "establishment". As a result, the pastoral attitude of the Church was mainly defensive and concerned with "keeping the faith". This sense of being a beleaguered minority helped to preserve the remarkable cohesiveness of the Australian Catholic community (62% of Australian Catholics, for example describe themselves as regular churchgoers. See also the recent sociological work by H. Mol, *Religion in Australia*, Melbourne, 1971). There are signs now that this cohesiveness is breaking up, because of socio-economic changes within the Catholic community—Catholics having moved from being predominantly working-class to being mainly middle-class—and a partial breakdown in the Catholic school system, which has hitherto been able to take charge of the education of all Catholic children from five to eighteen years of age (in Australia, universities are all state institutions and there are no Catholic or other denominational agencies of tertiary education). However, the full effect of these changes has not yet been felt within the Catholic community.

Like Australian society as a whole, the Australian Catholic Church has been in the past mainly oriented towards Europe, and it is really only since the last war that Australians have become conscious that they are part of South-East Asia and that their future fate is bound up with Malaysia, Indonesia, Thailand, India, Japan, and eventually China. The Australian Church, however, still has to come to terms with this fact. At present its whole outlook and its modes of thought are intransigently European and "Roman", and no real effort has been made to engage in dialogue with Asia and the religions of Asia.

Australian Catholics also share with their fellow Australians a basic social and political conservatism. Anti-Communism (usually with China in view) has been a powerful influence in Australian society and Australian Catholicism, and this has caused any attempts at social and political radicalism within the Church to be treated with suspicion. The *Catholic Worker* group, for ex-example, has been viewed unfavourably by a number of bishops, and the Melbourne-based peace association "Pax" has also been criticized for its opposition to the Vietnam war and for its attempt to promote dialogue with Marxism.

At the present time, contestation is not a major issue in the Australian Catholic community. Australian Catholics have not suffered the divisions and conflicts that have affected the Church in the U.S.A., and in some parts of Europe. But equally those creative tensions and dialectical oppositions that are an important source of vitality and growth in the Church have not occurred in Australian Catholicism. Perhaps only when the Church in Australia is forced to come to terms with Asia, and the great human and social problems and religious issues of Asia, will it awaken from its present state of pleasant torpor and become open to the promptings of the Holy Spirit.

Bibliography: For a brief survey see "The Catholic Church in Australia", *Herder Correspondence* (English edition), December 1966; the standard history is James J. Murtagh, *Australia—the Catholic Chapter* (Sydney, 1959). See also: T. L. Suttor, *Hierarchy and Democracy in Australia, 1788–1870* (Melbourne, 1965); John N. Molony, *The Roman Mould of the Australian Catholic Church* (Melbourne, 1969); H. Mayer (ed.), *Catholics and the Free Society* (Melbourne, 1961). For a modest attempt at Christian radicalism in an Australian setting, see P. Ormonde (ed.), *Catholics in Revolution* (Melbourne, 1968).

Karl-Behrnd Hasselmann

Contestation in the Evangelical Church in Western Germany

ONE of the first examples of the new modes of contestation in the Evangelical Church in the German Federal Republic was the conflict between the congregation of the Kaiser Wilhelm Memorial Church and the student church communities in West Berlin.[1]

The Evangelical Student Community (ESG) of the Berlin Free University, and later all the Berlin student church communities, had been active in the student movement since the summer of 1965. Their involvement had led to a succession of fundamental theological and political declarations which were intensively discussed in the Church at large. The conflict came to a head when, during the demonstrations against the Shah of Iran in Berlin on 2 June 1967, B. Ohnesorg, a student and a member of the ESG, was shot dead by a policeman. A situation resembling civil war followed, particularly on the campus of the Free University. At this point the Berlin bishop Scharf came out, surprisingly, in favour of the students, contrary to the opinion of the press and of the overwhelming majority of the ecclesiastical and secular public. In September 1967 the Berlin ESG applied to the parish council of the Kaiser Wilhelm Memorial Church to use the church for communion services. Contrary to expectation, this request was refused; the reason given being the political attitude of the student chaplains and their "parishes". This refusal led then to an "excommunication" of one community by another unique in post-war Germany. The conflict, now developing in

[1] Cf. K. B. Hasselmann, *Politische Gemeinde* (Hamburg, 1969), pp. 130 ff.

all keenness and with full publicity, rapidly revealed that: The catalysts of the inner-ecclesial contestations were the aims, methods and supporters of the student movement; the most important level of conflict was the local parish, with its particular way of going about things,[2] which was at variance with that of the functional parish of the ESG. A fundamental contradiction was revealed between the demands and the reality of the work of the parish which led to a striking polarization within the Church's work as a whole. This polarization spread into the administration of the Church, into the church districts and synods of the regional Churches and of the Evangelical Church in Germany (EKD). It led to the formation of inner-ecclesial pressure groups who now openly urged their demands, which had until then always been pushed aside by the "Pastors' Church". In Berlin and in other places, the contestations received immediate publicity through magazines produced by the groups themselves. The population as a whole was involved in that all the mass media immediately pounced on anything to do with the subject of "Church", even including "purely" theological controversies.

I shall now look at the causes, levels and settlements of the conflicts individually:

The causes of the phenomenon of contestation within the Church have come from outside; where Germany is concerned, the international student movement first took shape in Berlin.[3] It showed clearly that the post-war period in the Federal Republic was at an end. The students no longer had any concrete memories of the Nazi regime, of the privations of the reconstruction with its phrenetic search for prosperity and high production, and its inflexible anti-Communism, which restricted any free discussion. Intellectualism in general suffered under an output pressure and an urge for legitimation, which acknowledged only economic criteria. Public opinion was anti-Socialist and ostensibly Christian-inspired. Where it did not need the Christian fig-leaf, it was wholly taken over by blatant technocratic interests.

The rise of the student movement was almost accidental, but it

[2] First pointed out in E. Lange, "Ein anderers Gemeindebild", in *Evangelische Kommentare*, 1968, 2, pp. 75 ff.

[3] See, besides Hasselmann, F. W. Marquardt, *Studenten im Protest* (Frankfurt, 1968).

spread rapidly into all the social institutions, which had cast an ideological sheen over the socio-economic conditions of West German society. Now greater openness was insisted on, and in part achieved in regard to all the decisions of these institutions, as also control and co-participation, revelation of their dependence on economic interests and their involvement with certain power élites. A demythologization of the expert began: the relationship between professor and student, teacher and pupil, master and apprentice, doctor and patient, actor and audience, publisher and editor, editor and reader, lawyer and client, pastor and church-goer, was critically examined and recast. The result was and still partly is a general crisis in orientation among the population, which in the Federal Republic finds itself for the first time since the war at the mercy of a pluralism of institutions and values. This pluralism is, now as ever, the most convincing proof of secularization;[4] it is shown in the dissolution of cultural, ethical and social patterns, in the general mobility of individuals, in the varying rival roles of individuals, and in the varying rival institutions competing for the favours of the individual. This explosively widening crisis in orientation experienced by the German people resulted in a profound sense of insecurity, which is still in the main aggressively directed towards students.

From the start, the Church was drawn into this conflict, which also included the question of the Third World. After 1945, the Church had emerged as the only intact institution. It had the men whom everyone listened to. It was readily accepted by all parties and groups of the emergent prosperous society, and attained through this goodwill all the key positions which until today have represented the main links between Church and society: in relation to schools, universities, hospitals, institutions, the military, films, radio and television, taxation laws, general jurisdiction in youth welfare legislation and Federal social assistance legislation, penal laws, and so on. The Church carried a financial weight not to be ignored. Not to belong to the Church was, socially at least, a disadvantage. It was precisely this Church which proved during the course of the conflicts to be one of the

[4] J.-Chr. Hoekendijk, *Die Zukunft der Kirche und die Kirche der Zukunft* (Stuttgart, 1964); W. Jetter, *Was wird aus der Kirche?* (Stuttgart, 1968) (contains bibliography).

weak components of society; the still continuing movement away[5] from the Church illustrates this forcibly.

Now we come to a more detailed description of the levels of contestation in the Church. The real reason for its virulence is not simply a particular hierarchical grading of its competencies or an inflated bureaucracy. Much more important is the fact that in it a form of the Church—the parish—is declared sacrosanct which is in no way tailored to cope with the conflicts going on around it today. The parish is the classical achievement of adaptation of the Church to a stable, pre-industrial society in the fundamental elements of its life: village, market, small town. In former times, there was no social phenomenon which could not be dealt with in the parish. Industrialization, with all its consequent phenomena, brought about not so much a loss of, as a change in, the functions of the parish.[6] The living environment with the children, young people, housewives, ageing and elderly, and the socially non-integrated, remains the province of the local parish, and still places considerable demands on it. On the other hand most of the relevant realms of conflict, and thus the centres where social and political decisions are made, lie outside the competence of the local parish.

The source of all inner-ecclesial contestations of recent times is now quite clearly the fact that the Church authorities have responded negatively to the question of a political mandate—a mandate which they have exercised so naïvely and unthinkingly in the post-war period, and which has to be applied expertly in certain supra-parochial fields of decision—whenever groups in the Church have made use of it to criticize society, and even the Church as institution. The activities of the critical "functional parishes" and aid groups were then gauged according to the limited norms set down for the parish. In the Hamburg regional church in recent years, the student and social chaplains active there have been forced out of their work by the Church authorities, because they have acted so unequivocally within the field of their responsibility—something which the Church

[5] "Drei in seinem Namen—Gibt es Christen ausserhalb der Kirche?", editorial in *Evangelische Kommentare*, 1971, 2, pp. 65 ff.

[6] J. Matthes, *Die Emigration der Kirche aus der Gesellschaft* (Hamburg, 1964).

authorities and local parish representatives probably would not have been able to do.

Apart from these differences between local and functional parishes (mostly student communities), there have been grave conflicts between groups which no longer felt represented by the parish, and the Church authorities. In 1966, a group of Catholics and Protestants in Cologne discussed confessions of faith, and involved the political dimension of the Christian faith. This ecumenical group grew, and in 1968 organized, during the Essen "Katholikentag", a first "political vigil",[7] which in subsequent years was tried out in numerous parishes of other regional Churches as a new form of worship and action. The co-founder of this group, Dorothée Sölle, wrote in explanation of the vigils: "... a religious prayer without political relevance is hypocrisy. Theological reflection without political application is meaningless."

As a result, Cardinal Frings prohibited the vigil in the Catholic Church, while the Evangelical President Beckmann compared the group to the "German Christians" of the Third Reich. This accusation was later withdrawn, but the basic question remained: was the institution of the Church to become politically active as an advocate of the weak and oppressed, or was political involvement basically a matter for the individual? This conflict rapidly spread, with the help of the entire West German press, when at Christmas 1967 it came to a series of disruptions of church services,[8] which were continued the following Christmas. It was mainly young people who, following Rudi Dutschke's interruption of the service in the Kaiser Wilhelm Memorial Church at Christmas 1967, demanded of the Church a practical proof of its preaching of "Peace on Earth" in its actions, and wanted this question discussed in the service.

Contestations of a different type, namely within the parish, have occurred, for example, in Flensburg.[9] The provost and

[7] Dorothée Sölle & Fulbert Steffensky (Eds.), *Politisches Nachtgebet in Köln* (Stuttgart & Mainz, Vol. I, 1969; Vol. II, 1970).
[8] "Ein anderes Bewusstsein", editorial in *Evangelische Kommentare*, 1968, 3, pp. 121 ff.
[9] H. Fast, "Kirchengemeinder heute", *Lutherische Monatshefte* (Berlin & Hamburg, 1968), 12; *Zwischen den Zeilen*, 1-13 (Flensburg).

pastors of St Mary's parish in Flensburg were asked, at the beginning of 1967, to hold a memorial service "in honour of" the 86th Regiment, dissolved fifty years previously; the clergy refused to hold the service. There was a war memorial in St Mary's, retention of which was disputed in the parish council. The group which wanted it preserved got the better of the pastors. The refusal to hold the memorial service and the publicizing of the reasons for this refusal led to a commotion which caused the theological faculty and the bishop to vote against the pastors, and the then Federal Minister of Justice to vote for them. The fact that, on the decision of the parish council, the war memorial was after all removed from the church, hit a sensitive nerve of a bourgeois middle-class society. From the background of this apparently trifling matter the question quickly emerged of the justification and whitewashing of war by the Church. These problems were discussed for months in the press and on the streets—and not only in Flensburg. The conflict was aggravated when the Flensburg pastors began, beyond the borders of the parish, to involve themselves politically, and also ecclesiopolitically, in the narrower sense of the word, creating for themselves to this end a very successful organ in the magazine *Zwischen den Zeilen* ("Between the Lines").

A second plane of conflict was the synod. Here, too, Berlin was in at the beginning. When in September 1968 the synod of the EKD met in Berlin, for the first time a group of students, assistant lecturers, priests and congregation members was formed who followed the deliberations of the synod with placards, interruptions and discussions with individual synod members. Leaflets and sharp comments from the gallery, especially on questions of development policy and church development aid, unnerved the synod members to such an extent that they declared themselves unprepared to discuss the demands of their critics. The following synod of the Berlin-Brandenburg church, however, learned from these incidents; it included in its future deliberations representatives of the critical groups. But the spark quickly flew to other regional Churches. Thus the "Kritische Kirche Württemberg",[10]

[10] W. Simpfendörfer, *Offene Kirche—Kritische Kirche* (Stuttgart, 1969), pp. 77 ff.

a group of hundreds of "laymen" and theologians, took advantage of the resignation of the synod president Klumpp at the Autumn synod of November 1968 to support the democratizing measures the president had wished to introduce. In Württemberg it came for the first time to a discussion on the legitimacy of the formation of parties and groups within the Church, on a better Church information service, and election to ecclesiastical offices for fixed periods. These subjects were subsequently energetically championed by critical groups in the regional synods in the Palatinate, in Oldenburg, Bavaria, Brunswick and Hessen-Nassau.

These activities culminated, provisionally at least, at the EKD synod in May 1970 at Stuttgart, in the presentation to synod members by the ESG of a list of resolutions and comments which had in part been previously worked out. In the EKD synod in February 1971, members of the Study Group for Church Reform (set up in 1962) presented a systematic list of all their grievances to the synod members. The extremely liberal construction of their proposals for democratization differed not at all from the more "socialistically" conceived proposals of the student community. A synopsis of all the proposals made in recent years offers roughly the following picture[11]:

1. The pluralism of opinions in the Church is expressed in the formation of distinct groups; the tolerance necessary for this has however until now been neither theologically acknowledged nor exercised on the practical plane.

2. Group formations already have their place in the local parishes; they are mostly oriented to matters in which the "layman" knows better than the theologian. By legitimizing the formation of these groups in the parish many people would be moved to take part who at the moment feel patronized.

3. Co-participation in the church demands the foundation of a comprehensive information service and theological instruction for adults.

[11] W. Simpfendörfer, op. cit., pp. 84 ff.; Klumpp/Heintze/Schulz/Rau/ Lehndorff/Scharf/Beckmann/Niemöller/Brunotte/Linz, "Soll es in der Kirche Parteien geben?" in Radius (Stuttgart, 1969), 3; E. G. Mahrenholz, "Plädoyer für Gruppenbildung", ibid.; Ditzfelbinger/Dross, "Demokratie in der Kirche", in Radius (1969), 1; I. Stoodt, "Demokratisierung der Kirche, Wissenschaft und Praxis" (Göttingen, 1970), 6.

4. Greater participation in the decisions of the Church bodies demands a flexibly applied system of co-option, drawing in experts; the enormous advantage in information possessed by the ecclesiastical bureaucracy must be compensated by internal information services; a board system oriented to permanent technical questions is required, to offer expert advice to all the decision-makers; a strict division of powers is necessary in order to force the bureaucracy to carry out essential improvements and not to block them as they come into being; ecclesiastical offices, even episcopal office, should, like the synodal offices, be subject to a time limit.

These alterations in structure, to be carried out at all levels in the Church's work, are not for the sake of a smoother running of the apparatus, but for the sake of a comprehensive presence of the Church of Jesus Christ in the world, carrying out its task of being "the Church for others".

Meanwhile the regional Churches have begun to gather together the divergent and at times rival groups through the installation of structural committees, and thus begun to make them serviceable to the work of the Church as a whole. Thus the student communities are acquiring a new legal status as functional parishes. On the other hand an attempt is being made to strengthen the middle levels of Church work. There the functions which are no longer carried out by the parish are to be handled by specialists: advisory services, work with the young and the elderly, with marginal groups; local political questions, and so on. This strategy of settling conflicts has been relatively successful, especially as the social pressure of the critical and Left-wing groups is on the whole slackening off, and a clear move to the Right is emerging in all socially relevant institutions. Another symptom of a new situation in the Church is the relatively widespread echo which the so-called "Revivalist" groups have met with among the silent majority of the parishes.

In order to describe the great variety of conceivable fronts and bases of contestation, various typologies[12] have been attempted: traditionalists, representatives of the church-going contingent of

[12] C. D. Schulze, "Typologie von Kirchenreform-Bestrebungen, Pastoraltheologie" (Göttingen, 1969), 3, pp. 106 ff; K. W. Dahm, "Reform und Realität", ibid., 7, p. 297.

the parish (with its conservative wing in the "Revivalists" and its progressive wing in the "brotherhoods"), avant-gardists and the "Kritische Volkskirche". These attempts have shown that there is a theology of the parish to correspond to any concrete utopia of the form and structural possibilities of the Church. It could certainly also be shown that each individual type is allied specifically to one of the existent forms of the Church: the local parish, the functional parish (student-, pupil- and social-priest communities and parishes proper), the task force, which carries out a task for a limited period, and the Church authorities. Particularly progressive groups act mostly outside the institutional framework of the Church, and within short periods—for example, the pressure groups of theology students, curates, catechists, parish assistants, teachers of religion, etc., whom I have had to neglect in this article, as also the conflicts between individual pastors and their Church authorities, especially because of their refusal to baptize children, and so on.[13]

The attempt to bind the critical groups (even organizationally) more strongly together came to grief in the still existent "action for Church reform" over the argument that through this the spontaneity of the measures taken could suffer; in the so-called "Celler Konferenz" a more effective co-ordination did not come about because of the incompatibility of programmes (for the most part ideologically motivated).[14]

Contestations of the type described are a totally novel phenomenon in the Evangelical Church in Germany. They are an indication of secularization and its pluralizing effects; they correspond, often exactly, to related social and personal challenges and thus to existing non-ecclesial groupings. The Church has to adapt itself to this new situation. Various forms of parish and levels of organizaton, which in aims and possible forms of action differ and stand out from one another, must be conceivable in the Church. The tensions necessarily arising from this need not necessarily be solved by spectacular contestations; they can also be solved by technical discussion. What is lacking is a theology of

[13] "Aktion Kirchenreform Informationsdienst", Cologne, from April 1969: information on addresses and activities of the various reform groups.
[14] "Reformer zwischen Revolution und Resignation", editorial in *Evangelische Kommentare* (Stuttgart, 1970), 7, p. 381.

the parish which covers the social reality and shows perspectives of rival forms of parish work, and a corresponding theological self-understanding. Group formations in the Church, including the different confessions, would then not be a necessary evil, but a natural expression of Christian existence in the world of today.

Translated by Della Couling

Gerhard Schneider

Contestation in the
New Testament

IN German-speaking countries the term "contestation" has not yet become established. However, the latest German encyclopedia includes it, defines it as "the active questioning of existing structures of authority or society", and derives the word from the Latin and the French.[1] Occasionally in Germany one finds the French *"contestation"* rendered as "protest". For some time there has been some uncertainty as to the exact meaning of "contestation". I shall try to offer a more precise formulation of the term by way of the French and the Latin, in order to inquire into the New Testament use of the concept.

I. Contestation as Witness

According to the *Grand Dictionnaire Larousse*, contestation is "action de contester, de ne pas admettre, débat, dispute". The verb "contester" is explained as: "mettre en discussion le droit ou la prétention de quelqu'un à quelque chose". According to Larousse, it is a placing in question of the legitimacy of something or of the competency of a person. The use of the Latin root *"testari"* already indicates that a legal viewpoint attaches to the history of the word. In Latin, *"contestatio"* is a solemn calling to witness, an assertion made or decree laid down, also earnest entreaty, a beseeching.[2] *"Contestari"* means: "to summon as

[1] *Brockhaus*, vol. 10 (Wiesbaden, 1970): "Contestation".
[2] K. E. Georges, *Ausführliches lateinisch-deutsches Handwörterbuch*, vol. I (Hanover, 1962): *"Contestatio"*.

witness", "to initiate legal proceedings".[3] Without doubt, a corresponding legal motivation is at the basis of the biblical concept of witness and testimony. Jesus made "the good confession" before Pilate "in his testimony" (1 Tim. 6. 13). The apostles are, according to Luke, the witnesses of Christ who bear witness in the face of public opinion, and in contradistinction to the adversaries of the Gospel.[4] It is not for nothing that Stephen, who had to face death for his testimony, was called a "witness" (Acts 22. 20). In Paul, there is the linguistic equivalent to the Latin *contestificor/contestor* (συμμαρτυρέω: Rom. 2. 15; 8. 16; 9. 1). In this word the preposition σύν emerges more distinctly than in the Latin and French derivatives of *"contestari"*. The components of what is in common (to be co-witness, to co-testify)[5] occur in the Greek, although in the New Testament period the compound can only have had an intensifying effect. For Paul, it is essential that the verb refers to the testimony of the conscience (Rom. 2. 15; 9. 1), or of the Spirit (8. 16). According to Paul, therefore, contestation occurs not through the man, but through the conscience, which, like the Spirit of God, can give man a confirmation.

When Christians today refer in contestation to their conscience (or to the Holy Spirit), this corresponds with the Pauline texts. But it must be borne in mind that Paul does not base his own protest on the contestation of the conscience and on that of the divine Spirit, when he announces it. We know the scene from Gal. 2. 11–14 in which Paul opposes Peter "to his face". Here the "contestation" of the apostle does not occur by a call to the conscience or the Holy Spirit. It is more the case that Paul sets himself up in argument in opposition to the authoritative Cephas. How exactly is the "contestation" of the apostle in this scene to be understood?

[3] *Ibid.*, *"contestari"*. Cf. the Italian *"contestare"* or *"contestazione"*.

[4] See G. Schneider, "Die zwölf Apostel als 'Zeugen'. Wesen, Ursprung und Funktion einer lukanischen Konzeption", in *Christuszeugnis der Kirche. Theologische Studien*, ed. Scheele/Schneider (Essen, 1970), pp. 39–65.

[5] See F. Passow, *Handwörterbuch der griechischen Sprache*, vol. 2 (Leipzig, 1857), "συμμαρτυρέω"; W. Bauer, *Griechisch-deutsches Wörterbuch zu den Schriften des NT* (Berlin, 1958): same entry.

6—C.

II. The "Contestation" of Paul (Gal. 2. 11–14)

[11]But when Cephas came to Antioch I opposed him to his face, because he stood condemned.[12] For before certain men came from James, he ate with the Gentiles (-Christians); but when they came he drew back and separated himself, fearing the circumcision party.[13] And with him the rest of the Jews (-Christians) acted insincerely, so that even Barnabas was carried away by their insincerity.[14] But when I saw that they were not straightforward about the truth of the Gospel, I said to Cephas before them all, "If you, though a Jew, live like a Gentile and not like a Jew, how can you compel the Gentiles (-Christians) to live like Jews?"[6]

If we consider the history of the exegesis of these verses, in which the Antiochian conflict between Paul and Peter is discussed, we get the impression that Christian exegetes largely felt the conflict to be painful and therefore tried again and again to excuse either Paul or Peter. Anyone wishing to produce an impartial interpretation today, which takes care not to detract from Paul's report, should at the outset carefully examine the well-meaning mistakes made hitherto.

1. Exculpating Exegeses

Clement of Alexandria interpreted the text in such a way that Paul did not encounter Simon Peter in Antioch at all, but another bearer of the same name from the circle of the seventy disciples (Eusebius, *Hist. eccl.* I 12, 1 f.). The explanation that the argument between Peter and Paul was feigned, a mock battle, can probably be traced back to Origen (Jerome, *Ep.* 112). Augustine contradicted this solution, and most Latin Church fathers also interpreted the text more impartially. This passage in Galatians proved very convenient for the Reformers,[7] but in general their exegesis continued along the lines of the text of the Latin scholars.

[6] For the following exegesis, see also the commentary by A. Oepke, *Der Brief des Paulus an die Galater* (Berlin, 1957), and H. Schlier, *Der Brief an die Galater* (Göttingen, 1965).

[7] See K. Holl, "Der Streit zwischen Petrus und Paulus in Antiochien in seiner Bedeutung für Luthers Entwicklung", in *Zeitschrift für Kirchengeschichte* 38 (1920), pp. 23–40.

A judgment of the scene based on the assumption that the Antiochian conflict should be dated *before* the apostles' council,[8] ultimately has the consequence that Peter cannot be accused of any departure from their decision. It should also be mentioned that there has been an attempt to understand Paul in his bluntness and Peter in his fear psychologically, and thus morally to exculpate the conduct of both.[9] Correspondingly there has been an attempt to explain the decision of the apostolic council from a different political situation—that of Palestinian Jewry existing at the time of the incident in Antioch.[10] Around the year 48 the original community of Jerusalem would have seen itself called— not least because of the famine prevalent at that time, thus for "economic reasons"—"to acknowledge the uncircumcised Gentile Christians as equal". Now the original community was beset by difficulties in the fifties. Because of the progress of national Jewish Zealotism the Christians in Jerusalem and in the diaspora would have been "threatened and persecuted by Jewish chauvinists". For that reason a man like Peter would have to fear "the circumcision party" (Gal. 2. 12), while Paul, although aware of this threat (cf. 1 Thess. 2. 14–16), nevertheless, out of "love for the mission to the Gentiles" and out of a "readiness to suffer for Christ's sake", represented a view which admitted no compromise.

2. Brief Exegesis of Gal. 2. 11–14

That verse 11 begins with ὅτε δέ presupposes that this scene follows on in time from the apostolic convention (2. 1–10); for δέ is used here in the adversative sense, corresponding to passages 1. 15; 2. 13; 4. 4. This means: in contrast to the *agreement* of

[8] Augustine, *Ep.* 82, 11; also Zahn/Hauck, *Der Brief des Paulus an die Galater* (Leipzig, 1922), pp. 112 f.; J. Munck, *Paul and the Salvation of Mankind* (London, 1959); H.-M. Féret, *Pierre et Paul à Antioche et à Jérusalem. Le "conflit" des deux Apôtres* (Paris, 1955). For a criticism of this thesis, see J. Dupont, "Pierre et Paul à Antioche et à Jérusalem", in *Rech. de Science Rel.* 45 (1957), pp. 42–60.

[9] P. Gaechter, "Petrus in Antiochia (Gal. 2. 11–14)", in *Zeitschrift f. kath. Theol.*, 72 (1950), pp. 177–212; revised version in *Petrus und seine Zeit* (Innsbrück, 1958), pp. 213–57.

[10] B. Reicke, "Der geschichtliche Hintergrund des Apostelkonzils und die Antiochia-Episode, Gal. 2. 1–14", in *Studia Paulina in honorem J. de Zwaan* (Haarlem, 1953), pp. 172–87.

Jerusalem, in Antioch it came to *conflict*. In Antioch Paul opposes Peter to his face. For Peter is "guilty". Paul anticipates this basic assessment, before he names the details of the incident. In the overall context of the argumentation it is important for the apostle to show that for the sake of the truth of the Gospel he resists Cephas too. However, Paul probably could not succeed against Cephas and the other Jewish Christians,[11] or he would certainly have mentioned it in this connection. Why Cephas had come to Antioch is not mentioned. Nevertheless there is nothing to indicate that he appears as head of the universal Church for an official inspection.[12] In what way Paul offers resistance is not mentioned at first. But in verse 14 it becomes clear that he takes Peter publicly to task—an active "contestation"!

To begin with (verse 12) Peter had eaten with the Gentile Christians in Antioch. This also included the eucharistic meal. In Antioch there was consequently a mixed Gentile-Jewish Christian community. According to verse 13, the other Jewish Christians of the community (Paul, Barnabas and others) also shared this communion with the Gentile Christians. Perhaps, as born diaspora Jews, they had a more impartial relationship with the Gentile Christians. Perhaps, too, they drew the conclusion from the Jerusalem agreement, which at the outset exempted only the Gentile Christians from the obligations of the Torah, that Jewish Christians too need no longer fundamentally obey the Law. For Paul anyway in Jerusalem it was already in principle the "truth of the Gospel" which was at stake (2. 5). But apparently in Jerusalem the problem of mixed communities had not yet been examined.[13] Paul did not know the conditions of the so-called James clauses (Acts 15. 20, 29). Gal. 2. 7–9 gives the impression that the concept of enclosed Jewish or Gentile Christian communities and mission territories was still prevalent. James, Cephas and John are on the side of the Jewish mission. Paul and Barnabas are on the side of the mission to the Gentiles. Verse 12 recounts how Peter, after the arrival of the "men from

[11] G. Bornkamm, *Paulus* (Stuttgart, 1969), pp. 67 f.

[12] J. M. Gonzáles Ruiz, "Pedro en Antioquía, Jefe de toda la Iglesia, según Gal. 2. 11–14", in *Studiorum Paulinorum Congressus*, vol. 2 (Rome, 1963), pp. 11–16.

[13] Cf. Oepke, *op. cit.*, p. 56: "The Antiochian conflict shows the question ... in a totally new phase."

James" in Antioch, altered his attitude. These would seem to have been delegates from James who at that time led the Jerusalem community. Peter "feared" them. He gradually gave up eating with the Gentile Christians.[14] Of course the expression of Peter's "fear" is determined by Paul's accusation. The impression is gained that Peter acted out of personal cowardice. However, Cephas' decision would have proceeded from a politico-ecclesial consideration. Peter could have feared the break between the original community and the Antiochian community, and he would also have been concerned for the unity of the Church. Paul certainly judged this situation more categorically—on the basis of the "truth of the Gospel".

The rest of the Jewish Christians "acted insincerely" with Peter. Even Barnabas is included in this "insincerity" (verse 13). It resulted in a drawing away of the Jewish Christians from the Gentile Christians. Only Paul withstood this movement. In judging Paul's assessment of this movement of separation, it is important to bear in mind that he qualifies it as "insincerity". By this he means that a gulf existed between the conduct and the convictions of those who drew back with Peter. This gulf need not have been a conscious one for them. But it is clear to Paul, thinking on the basis of the faith in Christ and judging theologically. For that reason he must make it clear to Peter.

Apparently Paul did not recognize from the outset the significance of the growing movement of separation. Verse 14 begins: "But when I saw. . . ." Paul was probably able to see from the beginning what was happening in the community, but its *significance* only occurred to him at a certain point. He recognized that the Jewish Christians who were separating themselves "were not straightforward about the truth of the Gospel". According to how οὐκ ὀρθοποδ οὖσιν is translated (e.g., also: they were lame, they were not on the right road, they did not go straight), another, closer understanding of the question comes about. But on the whole Paul's intention in making this statement is clear. The Jewish Christians were not acting consistently with the Gospel. Verses 2. 15–21 make it, how Paul understands it, clear, even though this "speech" of Paul does not originate from the Antiochian situation, but is essentially directed at the Galatians.

[14] See the imperfect forms in verse 12b.

"For if justification were through the law, then Christ died to no purpose" (2. 21). Paul calls Peter to task "before them all", i.e., probably in the plenary assembly of the community. The public offence is publicly censured. Paul bases his argument on the fact that Peter, although a Jew, "lives like a Gentile and not like a Jew". It is noteworthy that Peter lives like a Gentile even *after* the separation. Paul can only mean by this that Peter in general ate with Gentile Christians, and would probably continue to do so in the future. Peter no longer feels bound to the Jewish way of life. What now happens in the community is consequently an exception and inconsistency conditioned by fear. The main clause consists then in the reproachful question which is intended to show up Peter's inconsistency. "How can you compel the Gentiles to live like Jews?" When Peter in Antioch departs from his decision of principle, which as a Christian binds him to Paul, then he contradicts himself. He compels the Gentile Christians, moreover, to keep to Jewish dietary laws. But not only that! If they want to share the table, the eucharistic community and thus the ecclesiastical community with Peter, they will have to accept circumcision and the whole law.

III. Main Features of the Pauline "Contestation"

To sum up, if we ask to what extent the Antiochian conflict between Paul and Peter contained elements of what today is understood by the term "contestation", then at the outset it must be said that aspects of protest against an established system or a ruling order were not in consideration. Cephas' action could, however, become "system-determinative". Peter did not appear in Antioch "as the first Pope", but his esteem among the Jewish Christians promoted their separation from the Gentile Christians. It should also be realized that we are only informed of the incident from Paul's side. For him, the Gospel was at stake in Antioch. Peter, however, reacted more "ecclesio-politically". History, as the clauses in Acts 15. 29 show, partially solved the difficulties of mixed communities through the expedient that the observance of certain laws was recommended to the Gentile Christians. The more Jewish Christianity disappeared from history, the less pressing became the problem of law. It can be observed that Paul was frequently regarded as an ecclesiastical outsider.[15] His gospel of freedom only sporadically and laboriously gained ground in the history of the Church.

In the Church of today confrontation is not infrequent between those who, with an eye to the good of the Church, plan and carefully consider, take measures and make decisions, and those who are not prepared for compromises, because they look to the Gospel and wish to act consistently with it, without diminution. Hence they must contest publicly—for the good of the Church and for the truth of the Gospel. The last group will in this—at least outwardly—frequently fail. But the confrontation is, on closer examination, not just between certain groups within Christianity, for example between Church leaders and the Christian people, it is at bottom a confrontation which involves every believer who on the one hand is active in shaping this world and on the other hand (under the Cross) has daily to live the truth of the Gospel.

[15] See G. Strecker, "Paulus in nachpaulinischer Zeit", in *Kairos* 12 (1970), pp. 208-16.

Translated by Della Couling

Marie-Dominique Chenu

Contestation in the History of the Church

TEXT-BOOKS about Church history have all too often drawn a hard-and-fast line in the classification of institutional and doctrinal matters; some are judged as in conformity with the truths of faith and the Church, others set aside as more or less schismatic. Such text-books, even in their lists of contents, seem somewhat embarrassed by the countless phenomena which fall outside the two categories, on a very mobile front, and in a third dimension that cannot be classified in terms of obedience or revolt, orthodoxy or heresy. This doubtless explains the shocked surprise many felt towards 1968, because of the spread of contestation within the Church: the phenomenon appeared as something altogether new, and thus disconcerting; the sign of an unhealthy crisis in the Church. The very word "contestation" began to figure in theological and ecclesiological book-lists, as in the uneasy allocutions of those in authority. In reality (as has been made plain by eminent historians of the Church, and of the Gospel in the Church) the phenomenon of contestation has occurred periodically in all the ages of the Church, in the context of both institutions and thought; and, more often than not, its presence, though accompanied by distortion and confusion, has been the sign of renewal at work, or of the timely discernment of a new problem.

I shall now give a summary account of some episodes that exhibit the typical characteristics—and the causes—of what is now known as "contestation". I shall confine myself to the precise meaning of the word as it emerges today in the multifarious movements, inquiries, discoveries and anxieties within the Church in renewal. The extensive pejorative use of the word should certainly not be ignored; but its specific, quasi-technical texture should be preserved, precisely so as to situate and qualify an almost uninterrupted series of phenomena which cannot be narrowed down to a juridical dualism of docility and revolt.

Without referring to the events of the old Covenant (the conflict at Antioch and the Council of Jerusalem [Acts 15], which constitute the major "theological site" of contestation in the conduct of the Church, is discussed in another article), I shall start by illustrating the permanent tension that existed, and still exists, between the Churches of East and West. In principle, the institutional and theological pluralism of the two Communities is acknowledged; but it is not sufficiently realized that this pluralism of itself brings about a continuous contestation, in the course of which even the most successful agreements are not achieved without misunderstanding and heat. Western institutional and theological history has been gravely defective from this point of view, positions specific to the East having been put to one side as mere variants or tiresome misunderstandings. Among so many events, culminating in the so-called schism of Photius, I would draw attention to two small episodes in which the resulting settlement left intact the heart of the problem.

The first affair is known and studied under the name of the Schism of Antioch in the second half of the fourth century. Two individuals were in conflict: Pope Damasus and the bishop of Caesarea, Basil, both qualified by their institutional and doctrinal repute. The question at issue was the choice of a bishop for the patriarchal see of Antioch. The local church had chosen the Armenian Meletius, bishop of Sebaste (369). But an extremist group, amid the troubles of the Arian crisis, had upheld the candidature of one of its own members, Paulinus, who was consecrated by the Latin bishop of Cagliari. St Basil held firm for Meletius. This action recognized the validity of a juridical procedure in a divided community; more deeply, it expressed in structural terms the living tradition of episcopal apostolicity according to a quasi-mystical notion of the holy hierarchy. The West, rendered insensitive to this spirit by its juridical mentality, upheld Paulinus. Damasus, tormented by threatening schisms and ill-at-ease in Eastern problems, granted communion with the

Roman Church to Paulinus. Basil continued to support Meletius, who was persecuted and exiled; he died (379) without having re-established communion with the Pope. It was not until the following year that the affair was settled: St Meletius presided over the First Council of Constantinople.

The second episode was no less significant. It concerns the use of vernacular languages in the official expression of the faith, and bears on liturgical pluralism. The Slavs did not take kindly to the use of the Latin language, a symbol of Western domination. The Moravian king Rostislav, in order to withdraw from Germanic influence, had asked the Emperor for Greek missionaries who knew Slavonic (862). The two brothers Cyril and Methodius, engaged for this purpose, undertook an effective apostolate. Cyril, thanks to an appropriate alphabet, undertook a Slavonic transla-tion of the liturgical books and the Bible. At first Rome approved of the operation; but soon, while protecting Methodius against the Germanic hierarchy, John VIII reproved him for his linguistic innovations (873). The archbishop (Methodius) went to Rome to exculpate himself from the suspicions of heresy linked to his pro-gramme. He won his case on condition that he would henceforth read the Gospel in Latin first, as a sign of communion. After his death (885), his achievements nearly came to grief, for Stephen V again prohibited the use of Slavonic. Methodius's successor and his disciples had to seek refuge in Bulgaria. This wretched ques-tion, which pushed into the distant future the Roman canoniza-tion of the two brothers by Leo XIII in 1880, is a living illustration of the problems and contestations concerning the expression of faith in the vernacular.

*   *   *   *

From contestation aroused by tension between cultures based on geography, I move now to contestation deriving from historic evolution in society—such as calls outworn forms into question, and with them the Church. There was a striking case of this in the West at the time of the general break-up of institutions and thought-processes roughly at the midpoint of the long period of the Middle Ages. In all domains, from the economic to the mystical, the twelfth century provided the stage for a "revolution" that was decisive not only for the immediate future but for the

"Renaissance" of the fifteenth century. With all the other areas of civilization, the Church too—not without a fight—underwent a deep and turbulent mutation. Not because its internal evolution was a mere reflection of external secular movements; but it so happens that, in accordance with the economy of the incarnation of the Word of God in history, Christian thought and life take over the new creations of human society as so many possible resources: the structures and the hopes, the spirit and the action. Copious matter for contestation here, if only in the quarrel between the old and the new.

For three centuries the Church had found its spiritual, social and economic setting within the structures and forms of the feudal system, whose organization was based on agrarian life and an economy of mere subsistence, and where, in order to overcome the unreliability of seasons and relationships, men "entrusted" themselves, body and goods, work and peace, freedom and management, to another man in whom, within a reciprocal loyalty, they found security and help in distress. This "lord", in his paternalistic benefits, manifested the stability of the divine order: in social relationships as in the forces of nature, the one and the other being thus sacralized. The monastic state, in the Church, idealized this human society and provided this Christendom with men able to enlighten and govern it.

In the course of the twelfth century, through technical progress and economic development, the over-production of ready goods set up a market economy in which the circulation of commodities brought about a mobility of individuals, with unforeseen social relationships. A new class came into being in which trade-associations or guilds had pride of place; with this accelerated socialization, free artisans peopled the towns, the nerve-centres of emancipation. Corporations, communes, and—soon—universities formed the networks of collective intercourse and commitment, and the "neighbour" took on a new dimension. Under cover of this transformation, which challenged the established order in Church and City, an evangelical revival resulted in a pullulation of fringe groups, suspect to the authorities, who found in poverty, the hallmark of their fervour, a radical criticism *de facto* and *de jure* of clerical and secular display. These new "prophets", from Peter Waldo to Francis of Assisi, set up forms of collective life in which the relations of the Church and the world were modified. The contestation they gave rise to is well known—from movements and positions which obviously cannot be denounced altogether as popular heresies. The contestation extended from criticism of Constantinism to the new theology, from the refusal of benefices to freedom for itinerants, from curiosity of the mind to the democratization of institutions. This was a terrestrial and eschatological self-confrontation of the people of God.

This contestation can be located on the centuries-old basis of the Gregorian reform which, in its fashion, had wanted to disengage the Church from its social and political load. With the investiture quarrel there had developed the conflict between the body ecclesiastical and the Empire, in the course of which not only was the freedom of the Church asserted (as against imperial manumission) but also a monocratic concept, as shown by the Forged Decretals, *Dictatus Papae*, and so on. The evangelical revival of the twelfth and thirteenth centuries, whose mood was very different, could not accept this triumphalist ecclesiology without contestation. Among various episodes there is the Bull *Unam Sanctam* at the peak of the conflict between Boniface VIII and the king of France, Philip the Fair (1302). The text ended solemnly with a dogmatic "definition" affirming that all politics was subject to the Gospel, the Church and the Sovereign Pontiff. Result: contestation. In Paris John of Paris, the director of the university college of Saint-Jacques, an eminent disciple of Aquinas and as such an astute observer of temporal autonomies —refused to acquiesce to the Bull and was dismissed from his chair, soon to be restored to him by Boniface's successor. As for the Bull itself, it was agreed then, as now, that the theological grounds for the decision, based on political Augustinism, could not compel recognition: particular attention was drawn to the debatable grounds and the obligatory conclusion. To see things in this way obviously constituted radical contestation.

*   *   *   *

Among all the events and all the doctrines bubbling up in the Church and in culture in the sixteenth century, two developments —namely the discovery of the New World and the missionary expansion in Asia—presented basic and far-reaching (as well as immediate) problems as regards the propagation of the faith, and hence the apostolic equilibrium of the Church in a non-Christian world. In America, the conversion of the natives had been organized by a strict understanding between the conquering princes and the missionaries from the old Christendom. This politicization obviously favoured the invaders, both for authoritarian proselytism and for economic colonization. Against this generalized collusion, contestation arose in the name of the Gospel and freedom. At his own risk and peril, Bartholomew de Las Casas immediately launched a violent campaign against this arrangement and, in order to exculpate himself, had to make several dangerous journeys to Spain to uphold the cause of the Indians against the traditional theology of Sepulveda. By a significant conjuncture of events, his Dominican confrère, a famous teacher at Salamanca, was just then working out a theology open to the new rights of men and to the spiritual and temporal autonomy of the natives.

In Asia, at the other extremity of the world, the missionaries encountered an ancient civilization with its own religion. This was a difficult confrontation in which perceptiveness was certainly not lacking, yet there was also obstructionism on the part of a supercilious orthodoxy. The story is a long one, but the so-called quarrel of the "Chinese rites" in the seventeenth century is perhaps the episode most fertile in lessons as well as grievous in facts. Was it necessary to consent to the observance of ancestor-worship, the religious expression of those family traditions that constituted the political texture of the country? Or was it simply an idolatrous practice to be wiped out, even at the cost of relegation to the fringe of the deep thought-patterns of the country? After interminable contestation, the condemnation of these rites in 1742 put an end to any hope of an effective Christian presence. The decision was not to be reversed until 1939. This was not only a quarrel about liturgy but about understanding the incarnation of faith in a civilization.

On this point, contestation again reared its head in the middle of the twentieth century. Against his superiors' wishes, Père Lebbe (1877–1940) demanded the basic conditions for an evangelization detached from Western categories and taking over the values specific to Chinese man. Opposed and exiled, the

Lazarist missionary was rehabilitated by Pius XI who, in conse-
crating Chinese bishops, prepared the way for the ecclesiology of
Vatican II.

*   *   *   *

After this brief reminder of various past events, no one will be
surprised at the consternation of ecclesiastical society when faced
with the violent mutations of the French Revolution (1789–95)—
less on account of its persecutions than of its ideology. The Church
hoped to recover its tradition in the French Restoration and the
Holy Alliance; it vigorously denounced the errors of liberalism,
of modern progress, and of democratic ideology. From the
encyclical *Mirari Vos* to Pius IX's *Syllabus*, doctrinal and
disciplinary interventions poured out, obstructing just criticism
of liberalism by refusing to recognize the signs of the times.
Throughout these years there were not only enemies to rise in
rebellion but, in all the local churches, contestators to call for
more timely discernment. The excesses and infidelities of some
did not prevail over the good sense of the many. Renouncing a
vindicatory presentation of unfortunate obstructions, Vatican II,
in recognizing the freedom of consciences, also recognized the
evangelical resources of the modern world and of the progress of
mankind.

*   *   *   *

We apologize for such a summary dossier. Its intention was to
show, by means of various major cases, that "contestation" has
been a constant phenomenon in the Church, so much so that it
could be regarded as the normal condition of faith at work in
concrete situations, where it has to express itself in docility and
apostolic action. This is not an easy or comfortable historical
interpretation: not only do ruptures threaten, but ambiguities are
burdensome, for people, for institutions, for faith. The development of the Church in a world in movement has always required
research and initiative both in government and in thought (research and initiative such as heavy-going sociological writings
cannot provide). The very mission of the Church, under the
inspiration of the Gospel, demands an implantation of this kind,
before any institutional phenomena.

With this dossier as starting-point, an analysis should urgently be made of the *causes* that give rise to contestation, legitimize it and delimit it. The cases I have cited point to various causes, whether in the domain of space, time, government or economics. Also urgently needed would be a study of *conditions*, not only on the part of the established authorities, but according to the very nature of the contestation which, under pain of being unfaithful to itself, should develop within the Church community: a socio-logical law which links up, for the Church, with the golden rule of charismata proclaimed by St Paul.

Translated by Barbara Wall

Peter Huizing

The Church and Contestation

1. *The Problem presented*

Confronted with the term "contestation", the first thing the lawyer will think of is *litis contestatio*, a concept deriving from Roman procedural law and taken over by canon law. A dispute arises between two parties. One of them alleges, for instance, that the other has injured him in some way and should compensate him for it; the second party insists that he is not responsible for the injury and has nothing for which to make reparation. The first party lays a complaint against the second before a judge, who requires the plaintiff and the accused to appear in court. The plaintiff has to state what claim he is making against the defendant, and why; the defendant states that he is contesting the claim, and why. This is the *litis contestatio*, the laying of a dispute before a judge, who is then called upon to settle it according to law. Both parties testify as to what they consider to be right and call for the judge to intervene and thus to endorse their testimony or deposition, as the mouthpiece of authentic justice. The Latin *contestari* meant originally "to call God or men as witness to the truth and authenticity of one's own pronouncements"; later, also to testify, to assert forcefully. The words derived from this in the Latin languages—French *contester*, Italian *contestare*—mean "to combat", to "dispute"—influenced, of course, by the sense prevalent in procedural law.

The expressions *contestation, to contest*, have acquired their typical current emotive value since the students' revolution in France, in May 1968. Instead of being an appeal to a universally recognized and operative juridical order and to the judge who gives judgment in the name of that order, this contestation is a protest against it and against those who represent and maintain it. The protest may be restricted to demonstrations within the order of law; but it frequently turns into an actual breach of the law and an attack on authority, possibly violent. The contesting group legitimizes its actions by an appeal to true justice, which the existing order violates. The group considers itself obliged to act as judge in its own cause, because no judge is to be found in the existing order who judges according to true justice. Every judge bases his judgment on the law as operative in the state—precisely that law to which the group is opposed.

In this number we shall be dealing with contestation as something that occurs in an ecclesiastical setting. This contribution will try to answer the question whether in a Christian community —and more especially in that constituted by the Catholic Church— contestation is acceptable, and if so, to what extent. It is at once obvious from the articles by Schneider and Chenu on contestation in the New Testament and in the history of the Church that contestation does occur, and warrantably, within the Church. The question raised here is how we are to decide whether particular forms of contestation in the Church are justifiable or not.

2. *Ecclesiastical Authority and Law*

A church as a community is subject to the sociological law that a society can have no existence without an orderly arrangement of responsibilities, obligations and claims, in short, without juridical organization; and that there must be bodies, agencies, which authentically establish and maintain that organization—in a manner, that is, recognized by the community—in other words, that there must be authority. Furthermore, in a Christian Church the structures of the legal system and authority should be based ultimately on the New Testament. Not that the New Testament can be said to contain actual concrete juridical norms, valid for all time; but even so, the structures it provides, such as the commissioning of Peter and the twelve, the organization of the local churches, the appointment of elders and presiding officers, the Council of Jerusalem and so on, do remain exemplary prototypes for Church law In the Catholic Church, the function of the hierarchy of Pope and bishops is the authentic implementing of the function of Peter and the apostles. They possess the authority to establish and maintain canon law on an authentic basis.

3. *Commissioning in the Church*

It is customary to say that this authority accrues to Pope and bishops by divine right. There is a proper way of understanding that, and a wrong way. A false interpretation would be that those who bear authority are accountable exclusively to higher authority, and the highest of all, the Pope, exclusively to God; so that the exercise of authority is in no way subject to the critical voice of the community, which is simply bound to accept and follow whatever pronouncements those in authority happen to make. But it *is* true, of course, that the mandate of authority in the Church is not given by the community alone. The community recognizes, or at any rate should recognize, that those who are selected for commissioning in this way are put into a position in which they are bound to act in Christ's name and interpret his authority for the community. Those who possess such a mandate know, or at least they ought to know, that they have to fulfil their function in the Church first and foremost in loyalty to him, and that they therefore receive that commission primarily from him. The congregation does not commission on its own authority but in obedience to Christ and in his service, in the knowledge that he is present and is at work in what the congregation does. The Church believes that this commissioning is sacramental, and it therefore takes place with laying on of hands and the invocation of the Spirit of Christ.

4. *The Authority inviolable*

For this reason, mandate and office in the Church have a certain inviolable or unimpeachable character. The community cannot of itself take away a mandate which it has given not in its own right but in the service and name of the Lord. The congregation cannot do what it likes with the (sacred) office. That office is "by divine right" in the sense that the office-holder is first and foremost one appointed and commissioned by Christ. This indeed applies not only to the office of Pope or of bishop. The baptized, the married, those who have been ordained priests—they all receive their mandate, their mission, as in the first place people commissioned by the Lord; and their function also is "by divine right".

A commission imparted in the Church is something on which God himself has laid his hand. It is fair to assume, therefore, that it is intended as something bearing "the marks of perpetuity". That does not serve in any way to show that no one can obtain a temporary mandate in the Church, for instance, up to a certain age-limit. A temporary commission would be just as much under the authority of Christ; and the person thus commissioned would be equally responsible to him in the first place—and the congregation no less obliged to respect this. What is implied here is that the position which someone occupies in the Church by reason of his sacramental commission, and the functions connected with it, are "hallowed" or "sanctified", that is, are placed in the hand of Christ and subjected directly to his authority, and so call for the respect and inviolability which are due to what is "holy". In the conditions of authority that prevail between human beings in the Church it remains true that the sole head of the Church is Christ.

But in the tradition of the Church this inviolability has never been envisaged in such an absolute and unrestricted fashion that those who wield authority are held to be in no way accountable to the members of the Church under their jurisdiction or control. Examples of limits set to inviolability are the traditional teaching on the "heretical Pope" and that concerned with "brotherly admonition".

5. The "Heretical Pope"

The adage: "The primary see is to be judged by no one, unless it depart from the faith" dates from the early Middle Ages.[1] Scholastic treatment of canon law further elaborated this principle. The prince of twelfth-century canonists, Cardinal Huguccio of Pisa (d. 30 April 1210), in his *Summa* gives lengthy consideration to the Decree of Gratian (c. 1140), from which it is evident that the question was being widely discussed already at that time. It became very topical at the time of the Western Schism (1378–1417). In those days apostasy signified not only deviating from true doctrine, from orthodoxy, but also deviating from the faith

[1] *"Prima sedes a nemine iudicatur, nisi deprehendeter a fide devius."*

in living and in conduct, from orthopraxis. The great majority of canonists assumed then, and still assume today, that if something should go wrong with a Pope, he can be deposed. They do not agree as to who is supposed to make the decision: some hold the college of cardinals to be competent, others the general synod or council—of course, without the Pope. The most orthodox school tries to safeguard the principle that the Pope can be judged by no one by saying that by the very fact of his scandalous and dangerous conduct vis-à-vis the Church the Pope has already abandoned his office; so that the cardinals or the council have only to conclude that he has ceased to be Pope. Hence they do not pass judgment regarding someone who is still Pope; nor do they depose him. Despite this construction, the fact remains that the right is ascribed to the Church as a body to pass judgment on the conduct of a Pope, when he deviates from the faith, and even regarding the termination of his office.

6. "Brotherly Admonition" ("Correptio fraterna")

Medieval scholastic theology was also familiar with an elaborate doctrine of brotherly admonition.[2] The doctrine amounts to this: that everyone has a responsibility for everyone else. If therefore anyone is able to deter another from committing sin or, by admonishing him, to bring him back on to the right path, it is his duty and he has the right to do so. It is not only superiors who have that right and that duty to those under them, and equal to equal, but also, where necessary, junior to senior, inferior to superior. In earlier times that right was repeatedly exercised, even with respect to popes, often by people who enjoyed great personal authority in the Church and by cardinals more or less in an official capacity, not infrequently in strong terms. The recent cases of contestation of the Pope on the part of a number of conservative cardinals are certainly to be explained on the basis of that tradition.

Both the classical doctrine on the "heretical Pope", and that regarding brotherly admonition, are based on the assumption that even ecclesiastical authority, the highest authority not excepted, is

[2] Cf. A. A. van Kol, s.j., *Theologica moralis*, Vol. 1, Barcinone, etc., 1968, nn. 245-8, pp. 228-30.

not shielded from accountability to the community and to individual members of it, at that. Criticism, protest and resistance to a wrong exercise of authority and to the upholding of bad law are things which ecclesiastical tradition has held to be possible within the congregation of the faithful—and has even regarded as a duty in certain cases, and thus as lawful and right. There is no call for us to alter this tradition because at the moment these things are described as contestation.

7. Legitimation of Contestation in the Church

Just as the mandate given in the Church as a community cannot be an arbitrary act on the part of that community, so criticism, protest and resistance to lawful authority in the Church and to canon law must not be undertaken in a highhanded, arbitrary fashion. Such protest is only legitimate if it has the assurance of being inspired by the Spirit of Christ and by his love for the Church. The right to protest in the Church belongs only to the person who is aware of acting by virtue of his own sacramental commission, in the Lord's name and on his authority. The office upheld by Christ is impeachable on one ground alone: because the office-bearer, in the exercise of his office, becomes disobedient to him. That does not mean that mistakes cannot be made in good faith and that when they are made we simply have to acquiesce in them; but contestation is not necessary in such cases. Protest is aimed at bad faith, if need be, at irresponsible, ostensible good faith, but not at honourable and justifiable convictions with which one disagrees. The fact that the person wielding authority goes against the ideas of certain groups, and possibly even against the ideas of a majority, is not in itself a legitimate reason for contestation. It may well be that in this way he is actually fulfilling his mandate.

8. Reform of Acknowledged Authority

Authentic protest is aimed not at the overthrow of authority but at its reclamation or reform. It begins therefore by recognizing the authority in question and showing respect for it. Where protest ceases to recognize the authority or where the protesting group disowns it, the issue is no longer one of contestation within the unity of the fellowship, of the community, but rather of separation or schism. In the Catholic Church, he who holds the apostolic office is first and foremost a guardian of the unity of the faithful, to whom Christ in his testament gave the command that they should all be one. The link with that office is no optional affair but one of the fundamental norms governing the structure of the Catholic Church; in the sense already indicated, "by divine right". The man who assumes a position of detachment from it stands likewise disengaged vis-à-vis the unity of the Church. He may of course say that he is breaking "merely juridical" ties, but that profounder ones still bind him to the Church—omitting to add, however, that he regards those profounder ties as optional too; for if he should feel that they *are* binding, he would then realize at the same time that of necessity they also create a legal relationship. The Christian engaged in authentic contestation does not usurp the position of authority; nor does he constitute himself the legally conjunctive centre of the unity of the faithful. On the contrary, he will be more than ordinarily sensible of the inviolability of the authority. Protest at the unchristian exercise of authority will only win the credence of the Church community if it goes hand in hand with respect for and obedience to that same authority.

9. *No Pressure Groups*

By "pressure groups", I mean factions which seek to force other people to knuckle under to their demands by means other than free persuasion. Those other means need not in themselves be violent in the strict sense of the word. They may consist, and do in fact consist, in large-scale manipulation, in various techniques of address, assembly and publicity designed to get at people and harness them to one's own bandwagon. What typifies manipulations of this sort is that their aim is not to bring others to insights freely accepted and to free, personal decisions about what they should or should not do, but on the contrary to render that impossible. The sole purpose is to influence people in such a way that they will do just what is required of them. We can see this happening on a massive scale before our very eyes: protest marches, protest meetings, protest manifestos, protest actions, where the marchers, meeting-holders, signatories and agitators are for the most part unimpeded by any degree of real knowledge.

In contestation as currently manifested within the Church, this same phenomenon is no longer a rarity, even if it usually appears in somewhat more subtle forms. Where it occurs, we need have no reservations about saying that such contestation is not an authentic aspect of the Church, nor is it authentically Christian. Protest which has a Christian inspiration also has as its precise aim and focus the freedom of the other party. It makes an appeal to his unobstructed belief, and to his free intention to act according to that belief. The contesting Christian is not going to effect anything with manipulation and coercion. If he opposes, it is not in order to repulse or put down the other party but to lead him into the same gospel liberty which he himself experiences. He takes no pleasure or satisfaction, even, in winning for himself a democratic majority in order to outvote the minority and in that way ensure victory to his efforts. He will go on, *with* his majority, to win the minority in freedom for the truth and for acting in truth.

10. *Real Contestation*

Protest in the Church will be directed not so much at people as at this or that state of affairs, not consonant with the Gospel, in which people are trapped and from which they have to free themselves. The protest is intended to prompt a radical change in people themselves. Therefore the normal form of protest in the Church will not be that of spectacular actions, accompanied by demands that everything which is wrong be immediately eradicated. Violent protests are hardly the way to set in motion the processes of conversion—certainly not conversion on a big scale; and that, after all, is what the Church is concerned with. For that, methods are required which call for more patience and can affect people more profoundly. Most, if not all, real reformers within the Catholic Church have been people who have come to experience in their own lives, and in depth, the truths and values of the Gospel which, as they thought, had been ignored. Their protest consisted not so much in a negative rejection of an unchristian exercise of authority and of injustice, but far more in a positive and intensified way of living *for* the Gospel. This—the most authentic Christian form of contestation—is coercive in one respect only. It compels people to take a stand and so reveals what is really in their hearts. The "advertisement" and "publicity" given to this silent contestation is often the counter-contestation of the people who are frightened of letting themselves be converted, and so proceed themselves to apply spectacular methods of compulsion and manipulation. The history of the conflicts between those charged with a charismatic and prophetic mission and those who wield authority in the Church teaches us how irresistible the authority of authentic contestation is.

Translated by Hubert Hoskins

Giovanni Caprile

Evaluating Contestation
in the Church

IN HIS speeches, especially since 1967, Paul VI has referred often, and sometimes at considerable length, to difficulties in the Church of today. These speeches already form a sizeable volume, from which it is possible to elicit Paul VI's thought on a correct and positive evaluation of these problems.[1]

I. Manifestations and Roots

Paul VI seems to insist on a necessary premiss: the roots and symptoms of this contestation must be exactly known. The manifestations he most often mentions, although with varying emphases and nuances, can be listed as follows: 1. *A crisis of Faith*, owing to a certain change in the direction of doctrinal orthodoxy, to the discrediting of tradition, to the anxiety originating from the rapid and profound transformations taking place in our world, to the lack of confidence (which the more destructive currents of modern thought have spread, in Catholic circles too) in the validity of the principles of reason. It is a dark whirlwind sweeping all before it, even faith in God. 2. *A crisis of authority*: the virtue of ecclesial obedience desired by Christ for the stability and development of the Church is contravened or denied; all

[1] In order not to burden this article with quotations, I would refer the reader to Virgilio Levi's *Di fronte alla contestazione: Testi di Paulo VI* (Milan, 1970). For the same reason I have only occasionally quoted directly from the Pope's writings even though I have been scrupulously exact in referring to them. Any document not included in the above book has been mentioned separately.

limitation and constraint is rejected in the name of every kind of liberty; it is affirmed that authority, being service, derives its power only from the base; it is not accepted that any normal authority, according to the established order, can suggest solutions and reasonable norms tested by historical experience; orders are received unwillingly, and deemed troublesome. 3. *A crisis in supernatural matters*: in religion, pre-eminence is given to the humanitarian tendency, i.e., a horizontal, philanthropic and humanist orientation, centring more on man than on God; Christian life is assimilated to profane customs; sociology is made the principal and determining criterion of theological thought and pastoral activity; it is affirmed that, to evangelize the man of today, a new Christianity must be fashioned, measured by man and not the authentic Word of God; only pragmatic efficacy is thought valid to measure the truth of Christianity and to make it acceptable and operative in a modern secular and technological civilization; and the utility of prayer, of mortification, of renunciation, and so on, are questioned. 4. *A crisis of structures*: A "free and spiritual charismatic" Church is set up in opposition to the institutional Church, which is said no longer to have meaning or usefulness; thus, confusedly, summary judgment is passed on both changeable and immutable elements, such as the hierarchical constitution of the Church, its doctrine, its teaching and necessary discipline condemning the whole past and accusing the ecclesiastical system of the past of every inadequacy and inefficiency in the expressions of Catholic life of the past; affirming the necessity to destroy structures, perhaps even violently, without having anything to put in their place, lacking authority and experience, unaware of how much is already being done, predicting innovation on which often mistaken or at least somewhat confused ideas are nurtured, or which would be quite simply destructive of the true Church of Christ. 5. *A crisis of union*: centrifugal and too individualistic tendencies; particularisms tending to absolutism, to the formation of sects, to detaching oneself from total charity in the name of a free, purely charismatic Christianity, for strange reasons, some perhaps good and austere, but outside the ecclesial context and thus apt to fall into decadence. 6. *A crisis of charity*: this is manifested not only in isolation from the Church, but above all in corrosive, unilateral and malicious criticism, isolated from the global vision of reality; this criticism sees everything outside the Church as beautiful and congenial, and everything done by Catholics as dull and blameworthy, uncongenial and intolerable; everything done until now as bad, and the upheavals advocated as all good, judging them "the more ingenious the less faithful they are to tradition, i.e., to the life of the Church; the more inspired the less they conform to the authority and the discipline of the Church; the more plausible the less they differ from the mentality and customs of this age".

Tracing these manifestations to the deepest roots of the phenomenon, Paul VI mentions: fundamental *distrust* of the values of reason, doctrine and tradition, distrust of structures, methods, men and inner values; a *craze for innovation*, a sort of passion for changes; a burning desire for things modern which is abstract, deprived of historical and psychological meaning, and not always tending to the good, indeed at times impelled to "envisage the hypothesis of a Church totally different from our Church of today, invented, it is said, for new times, in which all bonds of troublesome obedience, all limits to personal freedom, all forms of exacting sacredness will be abolished"; value-free innovations, conforming to the fashion of the moment; *a sense of doubt, confusion, dissatisfaction, instability*: owing to the conviction of the man of today, that everything is changing; made acute by the fear, in some, of being retrograde in the movement of ideas and of appearing behind the times or outstripped, by a painful inferiority complex, by a respect for humanity which most frequently ends in a dangerous adaptation to the spirit of the world "with a conformist and *avant-garde* zeal which can scarcely be called Christian", in "slavish and uncritical acceptance of the ideas of others". Often the pressure exercised by the mass media plays a part, as also the docile acceptance of superficial and fashionable phraseology, a confusion of the meaning of certain words, the establishing of certain pseudo-concepts. Finally, a *profound impatience, disquiet, haste, superficiality*: to the point of rejecting reforms, in favour of revolutions, of showing intolerance for any manifestation of calm, of gradualness and caution, which are considered signs of immobility, and adopting superficial, hasty and counter-productive procedures.

This diagnosis lends itself very well to a positive use: knowing the roots and the manifestations of the contestation in its various forms, one might seriously ask how the magisterial, teaching and pastoral activity of the Church should be planned in order to remain faithful to itself while keeping step with the world of today. An initial answer is given in the speeches of Paul VI.

II. A Calm and Objective Eye

Above all, Paul VI tells us to view the phenomena of contestation with a sense of proportion. He defines them, it is true, as his "crown of thorns" and does not conceal the profound bitterness they cause him or the injurious consequences he foresees in them, which would seem to justify a certain pessimism. But this is no reason to despair. They are basically "limited phenomena, even though real and not irrelevant", of a "crisis in growth". The Church as a whole is sound, all-attentive to post-conciliar renewal, wishing to render genuine testimony to Christ and to truly serve the world; "there still remains an immense majority of sound, good and faithful people" in whom one can trust, without "letting oneself be too influenced or intimidated" by the troublesome phenomena which take on serious proportions, but which "often spring from numerically small minorities and from sources very often not at all authoritative" and which are artificially blown up by the instruments dominating public opinion.

Furthermore, one must view contestation philosophically: it is the duty of the hierarchy to watch out for, but also to interpret, in the troubles of the Church, the positive and good sides, which can, "even in these disturbances and errors, be expressions of Catholic life", and which could be reabsorbed into a harmonious whole. Positive elements (as far as the Pope is concerned) are: the desire and the need for dialogue; the demand for more active and more spiritual participation in the life and worship of the Church; the desire for justice, for truth, for authenticity, for renewal with regard to real and long-established situations which are being put right; a fundamentally sincere zeal for finding new and more suitable ways of evangelization; a potential of forces and aspirations, especially among the young, which asks to be channelled towards a truly worthy, positive, constructive and inspiring mission which the Gospel is still in a position to reveal and to demand; a flowering of spiritual energies which should be viewed with respect and sympathy, because "they spring from reflection, from an awareness, from a gesture of liberation with regard to tired and now irrational customs, from serious purpose and personal commitment, from a search for the essential, from an inner scrutiny of religious expressions, from a trusting attempt to give to spiritual life a new language of its own and to theology some new and original expression, from some practical and courageous sacrifice which would give testimony of extraordinary Christian authenticity.

"All this merits attention and often also admiration. They are spring buds coming through fresh and vigorous on old branches considered incapable of producing signs of new life. They are precious energies, and the more worthy of affectionate regard the more often their source is ingenuous and young. Whoever has a sense of the psychology of the ideal rebirth of a generation, whoever is sensitive to the currents of opinion of tomorrow, whoever above all has a pastoral heart for the vicissitudes of the human world, cannot disparage, cannot ignore such pronouncements of spiritual spontaneity. . . ." Just as explicitly, Paul VI addressed the youth of Sydney: "The Church comes to you without complexes. It knows the values you possess, your strength in numbers, your enthusiasm for the future, your thirst for what is just and true and your aversion to hatred and to war, its worse expression, your rejection of the out-of-date elements in present-day civilization. God has put these values in you to respond with a new attitude to a new situation. There is an intimate connection, dear young people, between your faith and your life. For it is in the very dissatisfaction which torments you, and in your criticism of society—today rightly called the permissive society—that there is a ray of light."

In society, Paul VI continued, "daily more and more aggressive actions, new attitudes and models of behaviour can be ascertained which are not Christian. When you denounce them and ask society to reject them, putting in their place authentic values based on true justice, on true sincerity, on true moral rectitude, and on true brotherhood, you are certainly right. You have not only the approval, but the full support of the Church." One cannot "ignore so much generous and noble ferment in the present generation", without singling out "in the tumult of the disquiet and the present-day agitation certain aspirations, certain promises, which seem to me omens and factors of successful renewal".

III. LEARNING FROM CONTESTATION

Faced with this fundamental search for authenticity, with this "need for renewal which, for so many reasons and in certain forms, is legitimate and right", the third positive attitude to assume is that of humility. Such a vast phenomenon invites sincere reflection: the Pope and the bishops, who are so responsible for the destiny of the Church, must ask themselves how they can and must act to help realize the good aspects and neutralize the harmful ones, supervising and warning where necessary, without inferiority complexes or empty fears; but also ready to ask themselves with humble and absolute inner sincerity whether it has not been their own faults and their own "somnolence" which have allowed and shielded the origin of certain phenomena, some "failure in teaching" which should have been given, some incapacity in knowing how to distinguish the signs of the times.

To humility is added *freedom of spirit*: contestation, the Pope teaches, is carried out not only in the sense we call progressive; just as harmful is that of the "suspicious, of the critics, of the malcontents, disturbed in their piety", reluctant to accept any innovation even if it is authorized and justified, because they are nurtured in "distrust of the very actions of renewal of the Church", to the point of "confusing habit with tradition and of believing therefore that the Council should be considered closed and ineffective, and enemies of the Church those who promote and receive the new ideas coming from the Council".

IV. SYMPATHY AND UNDERSTANDING

Paul VI views contestation with sympathy, in the true sense of the word: that is, he feels the uneasiness which gives rise to it, and shows a sincere desire "to respond to it in the best possible way", and to receive "with loving attention" the voices and aspirations arising in the Church, "recognizing the constant need which our affairs have of being corrected and perfected; a need the more urgent the greater the modern demands for a continuous ecclesial renewal". Confronted by criticism and complaints, Paul VI tells us to accept them with humble and sincere objectivity, with a readiness to consider the plausible reasons for certain opposing attitudes, with a willingness to change what may reasonably be revealed as outdated or harmful to the best service of the Church and the faithful. In this he is supported by trust in the "depths of goodness" which is also in the heart of the radicals, in whom he is also quick to recognize "fundamental goodwill" and the numerous positive ferments which often lie at the root of their claims.

With these attitudes of mind, it will not be difficult to commit oneself to seeking and proposing valid and strong ideals. Sustained by the certainty of divine aid and the strength of the Gospel, one must have the courage to put forward to the faithful —laity, priests and religious—clear ideas and inspiring goals. Paul VI's speeches abound in appeals to the beauty and luminosity of the faith, to true love, total and active to the Church, to generous giving to Christ and to men, to a genuine commitment of conciliar renewal founded above all on exact knowledge of the Council itself and on faith in its validity.

V. SIGNS OF THE TIMES AND THE SPIRIT

In conclusion, in his speeches and by his conduct Paul VI has pointed out for us three complementary ways to make use of contestation:

1. To perceive it as a sign of the times: that is, an event through which the Spirit which speaks to the Church is stimulating us to reflect on our own responsibilities, and to act accordingly.

2. To receive these positive voices which "are coming to support the ancient ascetic wisdom of the Church", since "in some forms and in some profound motives of the present contestation there is perhaps a hidden rejection of conventional hedonism, of bourgeois mediocrity, of timid conformity—in this aspiration to a more simple and severe, and more personal, style of conduct,

Are our consciences not stricken by some of the austere claims of the young, such as sincerity in word and deed, poverty, liberation from the incubus of economic idolatry, and courageous attempts to imitate Christ?" And to receive willingly such entreaties, as was stated in the apostolic exhortation to the episcopate (8 December 1970), even though "they come to disturb our peace and quiet", to receive with patience, with a brotherly soul, with an open heart, "the indecisions of those who are seeking, groping for light", towards "all those who, deprived of this light of which we enjoy the benefits, nevertheless struggle through the shadows of doubt, towards the Father's house". And to take "part in their anxieties . . . in order to seek to heal them".

3. To profit, therefore, from contestation to help develop a new pastoral style, made up not of condemnations and anathemas, but of fatherly understanding, of patience, of forbearance, of sincere recognition of one's own possible failings, safeguarding the genuine purity of the faith and of those elements which God truly wished to be immutable and fundamental in his Church.

Translated by Della Couling

PART II
BULLETIN

Pedro Lombardia

Rights of the Layman in the Church

THE last few decades are full of evidence of the importance of the laity in the Church: the action of the Spirit seen at work in the lives of so many of the laity in their determination to fulfil a genuine role in the Church; the unquestionable richness of the doctrine of the magisterium on the subject of the lay state; an abundance of writings[1]; the general conviction that a Church expressed purely in terms of clerical functions belongs to the past. But the logical consequences of this development are still far from finding their proper echo in canon law.

There are a number of reasons for declarations of principles being out of step with concrete application: the caution of governing bodies, the anarchic and unconstructive approach of many protest movements, the vague "anti-juridical" feeling that has done so much to reinforce purely authoritarian attitudes without succeeding in legitimizing indefensible anarchies. ... This article

[1] The basic bibliography is as follows: *L'Apostolato dei laici: Bibliografia sistematica* (Milan, 1957); *Guide bibliographique sur l'apostolat des laïcs, 1957–61*, Supp. to *Apostolat des laïcs*, nos. 2 (1961), 1 (1963) and 1 (1964). P. Dalos, *Guide bibliographique sur l'apostolat des laïcs* (Rome, 1957). Dupuy, "Recherches récentes sur le rôle du laïcat dans l'église: Bibliographie organisée", in *Vie Spir.* 476 (1961), pp. 408–20. *Laici in ecclesia*, pub. by Laity Dept. of the World Council of Churches (Geneva, 1961). D. Tettamanzi, "Saggio bibliografico sull'apostolato dei laici", in *La Scuola cattolica*, bibl. supp. (1963), pp. 17–41. S. Larricia, *Considerazioni sull'elemento personale dell'ordinamento giuridico canonico* (Milan, 1971), brings the bibliography up to the beginning of 1971. A. del Portillo, "Los derechos de los fieles", in *Ius Canonicum*, XI (1971), pp. 68–93.

takes the teaching of the magisterium and recent theological thought on the function of the layman as its starting-point, and examines a few canonical questions that must be clarified if the rights of the laity are to be effectively safeguarded in the Church.

I. An Attempt to go beyond the Subject of the Laity

However paradoxical it may seem, I am convinced that lay rights in the Church will find effective safeguards only when we have convinced ourselves that the whole subject of the lay state is of secondary importance within the ensemble of the canonical questions that must be resolved if the Church community is ever to achieve a really just social order. This is because pleading for the rights of the laity is only meaningful in the context of a Church based on the clergy. Once the clerical structure of the Church is removed, much of the present rhetoric in favour of the laity loses its force.

The way the problem is posed at present still suffers from a concept of the Church stemming from Gratian's famous statement in his *Decretum: "duo sunt genera christianorum".*[2] Much of what is being said nowadays implies an acceptance of this division into two classes, and is an attempt to improve the lot of one of them: the laity. It is possible that this course will lead to a greater number of particular rights being recognized for the laity, but it will never lead to the final overthrow of a juridical image of the Church based on the class divisions of medieval society. A better approach to the problem would be to take the teaching of Vatican II on the essential equality of all the faithful as a starting-point, rather than the development of the rights of the laity, and to work out the canonical consequences of this common condition of all the faithful.

The objection can be made, however, that Vatican II itself requires a juridical distinction to be made between sacred ministers and lay people, by stressing the difference—"in essence and not only in degree"[3]—between the common priesthood of the faithful and the ministerial priesthood, and going on to point out that the organic structure of the People of God is "brought

[2] C. 12, q. 1, c. 7.
[3] *Lumen Gentium*, n. 10.

into operation"[4] through the sacraments, among which that of Order is logically to be included. So it is not surprising that in some sectors of the Church the only way to overcome the class concept seems to be through minimizing the difference between the two types of priesthood. So some would claim for the laity functions proper to the ministerial priesthood, such as the presidency of the Eucharistic Assembly. But there does not seem to be any doubt that, in the faith of the Roman Catholic Church, it is for the presbyter, by virtue of the efficacy of the sacrament of Order, to consecrate the bread and wine as a minister of Jesus Christ, changing it into the Body and Blood of the Lord. Obviously, one can preside at a brotherly gathering without this power, but this would not be the same thing as the Eucharist that Christ commanded the Church to celebrate as a memorial—a perpetuation—of his sacrifice on the Cross.

This brings us to the nub of the question: whether it is possible to have a canon law based on the radical equality of all the faithful—one, that is, that goes beyond the medieval view of the two-class Church—which still recognizes the distinction between the common priesthood and the ministerial priesthood, giving it the importance it ought to have in the organic structure of the ecclesial community. It must be possible; and to approach a solution in an orderly manner, I propose to divide it into two aspects, autonomy and public office.

II. Autonomy

Vatican II taught that the Holy Spirit instructs and guides the Church through a variety of hierarchical and charismatic gifts. The charismatic gifts in particular, it affirms, bring to their recipient the right and duty to use them for the good of mankind and the benefit of the Church.[5] These principles are essential for a full understanding of the deepest meaning of the juridical ordering of the Church, the framework in which the question of the rights of the laity has to be placed—if the word "rights" is to mean anything definite.

[4] *Ibid.*, n. 11.
[5] Cf. *ibid.*, nn. 4, 7, 12; *Apostolicam actuositatem*, n. 3; *Presbyterorum Ordinis*, nn. 6, 9. Also P. Lombardia, "Relevancia de los carismas personales en el ordenamiento canónico", in *Ius Can.*, ix (1969), pp. 101-19.

This does not mean that there are charismatic aspects of the Church existing alongside the juridical aspects, but rather that personal charisms also have juridical relevance, since the right and duty to exercise them follow from their existence. So canon law does not refer only to those aspects of the life of the Church that stem from official teaching, but to those that arise spontaneously from the initiative of the faithful. Besides the official apostolate, carried out by the hierarchically organized Church, there are private initiatives of the faithful, where they act "of their own accord",[6] the result of their own personal responsibility, which they need a degree of liberty to carry through. Canonically, this degree is defined through the juridical protection of the fundamental rights of the faithful, dealt with in an earlier *Concilium* article.[7]

The fundamental rights of the faithful are of course not confined to the laity, but belong to all those who make up the pilgrim Church of God. They are the rights that the Christian has, as a Christian, in the Church, and so belong equally to those who have an office within the government of the Church, not as the basis of the faculties necessary to perform this office, but for the development of that "personal condition of decision-taker in the ecclesial community, realizing the hierarchical effects of the sacrament of Order and remaining in them, clearly establishing the principle of juridical equality within the context of a diversity and hierarchy of ministries".[8] This dimension must be recognized as belonging to all the faithful for the realization of what has been incisively called "the apostolic spontaneity of the individual",[9] without which the Church, while remaining an organized structure, could not be a living organism in which Christ acts not only through the whole, but also through each individual member.

So the most important basic rights of the laity—the right to spiritual benefits, to the full exercise of personal gifts, to their own spirituality, to information, to free expression of opinion,

[6] Cf. *Apost. act.*, n. 24.

[7] "The Fundamental Rights of the Faithful", in *Concilium* 8, 5 (Oct. 1969), pp. 42–6 (American edn., vol. 48).

[8] P. J. Viladrich, *Teoría de los derechos fundamentales del fiel: Presupuestos críticos* (Pamplona, 1969), p. 367.

[9] J. Escrivá de Balaguer, *Conversations with Mgr Escriva de Balaguer* (Dublin, 1969).

etc.[10]—do not belong specifically to the lay state but to the common condition of the "faithful". The "two sorts of Christian" view of the Church has given rise to evident confusions in this respect. Canon 682 of the *Codex*, for example, defines the right to receive the sacraments and other aids necessary to salvation as one of the rights of the laity; taken literally, this could point to the picturesque notion that the clergy should not have the right to the last sacraments. *Lumen Gentium*, in tracing the development of the doctrine of the People of God, devotes Chapter IV to the laity, using this chapter to expound the doctrine of the common dignity of all the faithful and adding, significantly, to the passages in which it sets out the basic rights of the laity: "as... all Christians".

III. Public Office

Does this radical equality of the common condition of all the faithful also apply to the government of the Church? What relevance does the distinction between the common priesthood and the ministerial priesthood have to the exercise of public office in the ecclesial community?

When the Church is affirmed to be a hierarchical society by divine right, different aspects of the Church are stressed, and these should, strictly speaking, be kept separate:

1. The Church is an organically structured society that, by its very nature, requires a hierarchical organization with its consequent functions of government and holding of office.

2. Certain functions within the government of the Church belong to individuals who have received the sacrament of Order: the Roman pontiff as universal primate, for example, or the diocesan bishop as head of each local Church.

3. As the presbyters—and the deacons, by extension—co-operate with the local bishop, this co-operation must in some way extend into the governing function, which is one aspect of the bishop's position as head of the local Church.[11] But it in no

---

[10] The rights expressly recognized in the Council documents have been studied by A. del Portillo in *Fieles y laicos en la Iglesia: Bases de sus respectivos estatutos jurídicos* (Pamplona, 1969), pp. 90 ff.

[11] Cf. J. Souto, "La potestad del obispo diocesano", in *Ius Can.*, VII (1967), pp. 365-449.

way follows from this that every sacred ministry necessarily has governing functions in the strict sense attaching to it.

A separate aspect is that when certain faithful receive the sacrament of Order and so become either bishops, presbyters or deacons, they are thereby constituted ministers of Jesus Christ with regard to particular functions relative to the liturgical proclamation of the Word of God, the official preaching of the Gospel and the performance of sacramental rites. The laity are clearly not ministers of Jesus Christ in these respects, and so are not capable of exercising these functions. This is the most typical example of the difference between ministerial priesthood and common priesthood. This difference, besides its essential, onto-logical aspects, implies a distinction indicated by the idea of degree or hierarchy—a hierarchy of order—to emphasize the particular dignity attaching to ministers of Jesus Christ in rela-tion to those who are not ministers, and also the differences between sacred ministers arising from the varying degrees of dignity attaching to the ritual functions belonging to each degree of the sacrament of Order.

Therefore one can talk of those who form part of the Sacred Hierarchy (in the theological sense), of those who do not form part of it, and of differing degrees of hierarchy: bishops, pres-byters and deacons. The concept of power is frequently used in referring to the faculties ontologically possessed by the persons of ministers, including, in the case of bishops and presbyters, the power to change the bread and wine into the Body and Blood of the Lord. The importance of this hierarchy, one of whose greatest riches lies in this power over the Body of the Lord, for the life of the pilgrim Church, does not need any special pleading. For the sake of clarity, however, it should be said that the terms "power" and "hierarchy" are not used in this context in a technical or juridical sense, but by analogy, as theology often needs to use the terminology of other branches of learning to find some expression for what, as a mystery, is by definition impossible to express exactly in human language.

This said, it is important to point out that even though what theology calls "Sacred Hierarchy" or the "Power of Order" is something really essential to the Church, it does not follow that this exhausts the subject of public office in the Church, since the fact of being ordained presbyter or bishop does not necessarily confer supremacy of government over the rest of the faithful, requiring their obedience. It does, however, have a more important corollary: the faithfulness of Christ himself to his own Word, pronounced by his ministers.

To return to the technical and juridical aspect of the matter: it seems necessary to introduce a distinction between two aspects of the problem, while not forgetting the connections between them established by the will of Christ himself. Canonical science, at the point it has now reached, requires that we distinguish, following Hervada,[12] between Sacred Hierarchy—that Hierarchy of ministry with which theology is concerned—and ecclesiastical structure, understood as "the organic ordering of the official and public dimension of the Church".[13] This is the crux of the matter, because even if it is clear that ecclesiastical organization possesses some irreformable aspects *"iure divino"*, precisely by virtue of those functions that belong to the Sacred Hierarchy within it, it is equally clear that ecclesiastical organization is a wider concept. To equate ecclesiastical organization with Hierarchy in the theological sense would be equivalent to conceiving the organic structure of the Church as that of a society governed by those who have received Holy Orders, a society characterized by the existence in its midst of a *"coetus"*, *"ordo"* or "class" formed by its ministers —the clergy—reserving to itself all or at least most of the posts in its government. This would be a return to the idea of two kinds of Christian, to the classical, stratified concept of the Church which is in no way postulated in its divine foundation and is certainly incompatible with the principle of the radical equality of all the faithful, based on the common dignity of all Christians.

Once we have gone beyond a clerical conception of Church organization, the attitude that seeks to claim all levels of public office in the Church for the laity is also outdated, as this is as class-based as the attitude it seeks to replace. The solution to the problem lies in positing the basic qualification for active participation in the government of the Church as being not clerical or lay,

---

[12] Hervada-Lombardia, *Los derechos del pueblo de Dios* (Pamplona, 1970), pp. 329 ff.; see also J. Souto, "Consideración unitaria de la organización eclesiástica", in *Ius Can.*, ix (1969), pp. 157–78.

[13] Hervada-Lombardia, *op. cit.*, p. 330.

but simply participating in the common condition of the faithful. This principle would operate except when divinely instituted diversity of ministries required an exception to be made.

A full appreciation of the benefits this approach would bring would require a detailed analysis of the various questions raised by its practical application in relation to the different aspects of its operation: public opinion, sharing in the election of pastors, subsidiary offices, supplementary offices, etc.[14] Lack of space prevents me from examining more than one aspect of the matter here: that of qualification for holding office in the official governmental structure of the Church.

Vatican II gave explicit recognition to the ability of the laity to carry out certain ecclesiastical offices (*munera*),[15] in a text whose historical antecedents I have attempted to trace elsewhere.[16] This text, taken literally, makes two main points: one, that lay people can hold office in the official organization of the Church; two, that their ability to do so is limited, since it applies not to all offices, but only to some. Exactly which offices might be held by lay people was something that the Council did not attempt to define, but the principles already stated can give us an answer. Lay people can carry out any function in the Church for which faculties derived from the ministerial priesthood are not required. Seen in this light, there is no difficulty in stating that most functions in the official government of the Church could be carried out by lay people, without blurring the sacramental roots of Church structure, and without endangering the eminently pastoral orientation that Church government should possess.

Offices that have to be performed by people who form part of the Sacred Hierarchy in its theological sense can be defined as the following: Bishop of Rome, which carries the universal primacy with it; head of the local Church, for which episcopal consecration is necessary; and all those positions traditionally defined as belonging to the "cure of souls", positions that imply duties connected with the celebration of the Eucharist and the administering of the sacraments. So the *"munera ecclesiastica"* that remain open

[14] *Ibid.*, pp. 394 ff.

[15] *Lumen Gentium*, n. 33.

[16] *Los laicos*, not yet published, based on the Acts of the International Canon Law Congress held in Rome in Jan. 1970.

to lay people are by no means confined to secondary offices connected with the liturgy, such as reader, to participation in various
advisory bodies or in the administration of Church property.
There is, on the contrary, nothing to prevent a future reorganization of Church government giving lay people posts such as that at
present occupied by the Cardinal Secretary of State, Prefect of a
Dycastery of the Roman Curia, Nuncio, or judge in any
ecclesiastical court, since the suitability of candidates for these
posts in no way depends on whether they are ordained bishops or
presbyters, but on whether they have the right technical qualifications, and other suitable attributes of character, such as probity,
prudence, etc. Obviously, the exercise of these functions must
remain related to the sacramental roots of the organization, not
because those who perform them should receive Holy Orders, but
because they are exercised in the name of the Pope and the
diocesan bishops.

*   *   *   *

I hope these considerations have served to illumine the more
strictly canonical aspects of this problem. It cannot, of course, be
fully dealt with without considering its impact on the relationship
between the Church and the world, but this interesting aspect of
the subject is one that I have no space to examine here.

Translated by Paul Burns

Peter Huizing

The Revision of Canon Law

SINCE 1969 the papal commission for the revision of canon law has brought out several *Communicationes*—Reports—summarizing, among other things, the work being done by the commission's advisers in their study groups. At the time of writing there are to hand four of these reports; and I propose to give here a brief survey of their essential contents. We shall continue subsequently to follow the progress of these reports and the reactions they evoke.

1. *Basic Statutory Provisions regarding the Faithful*

The study group "On the laity and the associations of the faithful" has devised a scheme in three parts. The first part comprises basic law concerning the faithful and their status. A general section on all the faithful properly serves as prelude to a separate section on the laity. Hence Chapter 2 of *Lumen Gentium* also deals first with the People of God, which includes all believers, and then with the separate "states" of the clergy, laity and religious. All the faithful, when it comes to their dignity as human beings and Christians, their vocation to holiness and the duty, common to all, to fulfil together the missionary task of the Church, share a fundamental equality. By virtue of divine law, both positive and natural, there derive from this rights and duties which positive human law is bound to recognize and safeguard.

The scheme proffers in the first place a definition of the concept "believer"; a statement that this section applies to all; a declaration of the fundamental equality of all. Further provisions relate, for instance, to: the duty to maintain what is acknowledged to be the true faith; the right and duty to acquire such knowledge as is applicable to each person's condition; the right to free inquiry and the free expression of opinion by those engaged in the pursuit of knowledge in its various branches within the Church, having due regard to necessary prudence and deference towards the magisterium; the right to the spiritual ministrations of the Church, in particular, preaching and sacraments; the right to pursue one's own style of spiritual life and experience, as an individual or corporately, provided it be consonant and agreeable with the Church's doctrine; the duty to accept obediently what the authorities, as instructors and administrators, may teach and decide; the right to retain one's own rite; the right to participate actively in liturgical celebrations and observances; the right to help and share in the proclamation of the Gospel; the right to make one's needs and desires known to higher authortiy; the right to a legitimate and openly held viewpoint within the Church; the right to freedom from any form of coercion in the choice of a state of life; the right to association; the right to be held in good repute.

Likewise affirmed is the entitlement to defend one's own rights, vis-à-vis authority as well as in due process of law. Everyone has a right to be heard; to have defence counsel; to know, when a charge results in action or legal proceedings being taken, the name of the complainant; to know the arguments on which the decision or sentence is based; not to be penalized, save by reason of infringements as defined by law, and then with a penalty specified by the aforesaid law.

2. The Law as it pertains to the Laity

The second part of the scheme deals with rights and duties relating exclusively to lay people and with a number of general rights and duties in so far as they apply to the laity.

The peculiar missionary task of the lay person is to attend to various matters of concern in the world, in accordance with the order appointed by God. From this the layman's proper rights and duties derive. In this context he has his own responsibility and freedom, making due allowance, of course, for what is taught by the hierarchy regarding faith and morals. The autonomy of

the secular order is to be respected. The rights and duties which
lay people have as members of the Church are distinct from those
they have as members of society. The latter fall not under
canonical norms but under civil law.

To obviate uncertainty, certain general rights and duties per-
taining to the laity are affirmed: such as the right at an academic
level to study and teach the various ecclesial branches of knowledge and disciplines; the competence to be consulted as experts
or advisers by authority; the duty and the right to fulfil their
apostolate, individually or corporately; the competence to be
called to collaborate with the hierarchical apostolate and to be
appointed to certain offices within the Church.

This statutory provision contains general norms only. They
have to be made operational through their concrete application in
other parts of canon law concerning the participation of lay
people in Church government, judicial administration, control of
assets and so on.

3. Right of Association

The third part of the scheme contains some general provisions
regarding associations of the faithful; to supersede canons 684–
725 of the ecclesiastical code, which refer only to a few associations of lay people that have no existence in law, even, unless they
have been constituted, or at any rate approved, by higher authority.
The scheme recognizes the right of all the faithful, whether lay
or clerical, to establish and administer corporate bodies, proper
regard being had to a rightful relation to authority.

Canon law divides up these associations according to their ends
and purposes: tertiaries emulate the spiritual life of a particular
order; societies of the devout practise certain forms of piety or
charity; fraternities concern themselves especially with public
worship. These are all divided by the scheme according to the
relationship they have to the hierarchy: associations created and
run by church members, which come under the general super-
vision of the authorities only in matters of faith and morals, as
individuals do; associations set up or officially approved by the
authorities and more dependent on them.

The existing norms enter into far too much detail. They were
already inadequate even for the forms of association which

appeared not long before, or soon after, the introduction of the code in 1918. The present scheme confines itself to a few general principles; everything else is left to the local law and statutes of the several associations. In that way plenty of room remains for forms of association to go on developing, whilst clashes between "charisma" and "institution" are avoided.

4. Penal Law

It is proposed that *De delictis et poenis* be replaced by *Ius poenale*. The scheme proffered by this study group divides into a general section: offences in general, penalties in general, particular penalties; and a special section on specific offences. The general section is thought to be necessary because universal norms are indispensable for a right application of penal law, the fundamental norms must be uniform for the whole (Latin) Church; and such an enormous task cannot be assigned to bishops or their conferences. The scheme provides a legal framework for making and imposing penal legislation in the various churches. The special section covers offences for which an identical penalty, valid for the Church as a whole, is deemed opportune.

In principle, penal law is a matter of public order. Even here pastoral considerations must be paramount and the protection of personal rights assured. Non-Catholic Christians do not come under canonical sanctions, unless a particular law or prescript determines otherwise. There are various norms aimed at limiting penalties: the severest penalties can be exacted and imposed only by the highest authority; the penalty is to be imposed only if there are no other ways to remove the cause of offence, make restitution and reform the guilty party, and if this can be attained through punishment; the penalties incurred by the actual breach of law—*poenae latae sententiae*—are very much reduced and may be applied by the lower authority only in exceptional cases; for breaches of general law, the lower authority may exact an additional penalty only where the need to do so is extreme; when there are mitigating circumstances, the judge may dispense with the imposition of a penalty and take other measures or may urge the same upon the authorities. Even when a penalty is deemed necessary, as much pastoral help as possible should be offered the party undergoing punishment.

More comprehensive norms are suggested for a regulation or provision with the threat of a penalty attaching to it—*praeceptus poenale*—(as distinct from a *decretum*, whereby a penalty is imposed or it is declared that a penalty is operative without judicial proceedings). It is laid down who is able to make such a provision; that penalties permanently attaching thereto and indeterminate penalties be ruled out; precautions and formalities regarding the enactment and its disclosure to those concerned; the consequences of an appeal against the regulation.

Where liability is concerned, it is proposed that it be possible to punish only the person who has acted with intent, unless law or prescript determine otherwise. "Intention" is a conscious desire to infringe the law or prescript, as in canon 2200, par. 1. The idea of intention without any diminution of responsibility—*dolus plenus*—in canon 2200, par. 2, is dropped. The presumption of intention in canon 2200, par. 2, is replaced by a presumption of liability; one can surely assume that someone is responsible for his actions, but not that there is a deliberate intent to infringe the law or prescript. The presumption must yield not only to proof of the contrary but also when the latter is probable. Canons 2201–2208 are replaced by a general definition of the circumstances which rule out responsibility for the offence or, in general, punishable liability or which lessen or aggravate the seriousness of the offence. The norms bearing on attempted and frustrated offences are toned down: no penalty is affixed to them—only optional penances or punitive measures—except in very serious cases; and even then the punishment is optional.

Censures are retained, albeit in an attenuated form. A penalty ceases when because of a later law the penal law, or at any rate the penalty, is rescinded, even—in contrast with canon 2226, par. 3—if the censure has already been incurred. An appeal against a decree by which a censure is imposed renders the decree for the time being inoperative. Excommunication and personal interdict no longer involve a ban on obtaining sacramental absolution of sins; a far-reaching proposal for keeping the realm of conscience and confession separate from that of public order and punishments. Abandoned, too, is the rule inhibiting the excommunicated from receiving the sacraments (canon 2260, par. 1), and the stipulation that they have no share in indulgences, inter-cessions and the public prayers of the Church (canon 2262, par. 1). No censure may be imposed or said to be entered upon where the delinquent is not known. Likewise allowed to lapse are the censure of a community, the general interdict and the notion of ex-communicated people who are to be shunned (*excommunicati vitandi*). An excommunicated or suspended cleric is permitted to exercise his power of consecration and jurisdiction if this is neces-sary for any of the faithful who find themselves in mortal peril and always if and when they request it. Suspension and interdict are only censures, not "expiatory punishments" (the term "retribu-tive penalties"—*poenae vindicativae*—is replaced by "expiatory penalties"—*poenae expiatoriae*—following Augustine, *De civitate Dei* 21, 13). Other penalties abandoned here include those of infamy—*infamia*, the ban on a church burial, the removal or dissolution of an episcopal see or a parish, the ban on receiving the sacraments.

No censure prohibits the receiving of sacramental absolution. Confessors no longer need, therefore, to absolve from censures; nor do they any longer have authority to suspend an "expiatory penalty". For that reason it is proposed that the law itself should define in what instances the obligation to carry out the penalty is suspended.

The special section on breaches of general law contains: (1) offences against the religion and unity of the Church; (2) offences against ecclesiastical authority and the freedom of the Church; (3) usurpation of ecclesiastical offices and offences in the exercise thereof; (4) forgery; (5) breaches of particular obliga-tions; (6) offences against the life and liberty of the person; (7) a universal norm (not further defined in the report).

5. The Institutions of Perfection—"Institutiones perfectionis"

These comprise all those institutions, recognized by the Church, in which the members bind themselves, in one form or another, to keep the three evangelical counsels. Some introductory defini-tions serve to delimit the concept of these institutions and their constituent parts. Here are expressed the theological aspects of the consecrated, religious life, its charismatic nature and the

9—c.

special calling it entails; and its connection with the Church's mission.

A general section, relevant to all institutions, deals with the founding, uniting and terminating of institutions, provinces and houses; their relations with ecclesiastical authority; administration; control of assets; the admission of members and their training; the obligations of institutions and their members; ending of membership by transfer to another institution, resignation or dismissal. A special section deals with monastic institutions; institutions of religious with an avowed apostolic purpose, whether of clergy or laity; institutions having a common life; secular institutions; exempt institutions. There is no difference in autonomy between institutions of men and of women. The scheme aims only at suggesting indispensable norms of general law and at leaving some room in the institutions' own legal regulations for continual adaptation. The scheme proposes an ordering in detail of internal autonomy and relations with the central and local authorities. The consequences of exemption, as a peculiar legal status conferred by the pope, are dealt with in the special section. The purpose of the norms concerning administration and government is to ensure that these stimulate the co-operation of the members. The regulation of jurisdiction over the confessional, especially for female religious, is simplified. The general law has no fixed articles regarding the postulant. The conditions required for a duly validated novitiate and entry are reduced in number, those governing admissibility cease to operate.

6. Law of Procedure

The scheme proposed by this study group is intended to ensure greater legal security for every member of the Church through a prompt and reliable administration of justice. Judges are not to be discharged just as bishops may see fit. Proceedings should if possible be adapted to conform with the civil law of the locality; but there is still a need for an essentially uniform system of ecclesiastical suits in view of the hierarchical structure of the judicial bench and the right of every person to submit his case to Rome.

A lay person may be appointed assessor—counsel to a sole presiding judge; or auditor—clerk to an investigating judge.

Bishops' conferences may allow that in actions for the annulment of marriages one of the three judges in the first instance be a layman, when three clerics are not available for the regional court. They can establish regional courts of law; make statutory regulations about the organization of such courts and the personnel; set up boards to regulate a *modus operandi*.

Non-Catholics may appear as plaintiffs in contentious actions. Women may be admitted as counsel. Lawyers, but not the parties, may be present at the interrogation of witnesses, unless the judge determine otherwise. The interrogation is to be conducted by the judge, even when questions are submitted by counsel or the *defensor vinculi*, unless the bishops' conference decide otherwise. Cases in which the verdict of a court may be nullified are much reduced.

For actions concerned with the nullity of marriages, the competent body is the court of the locality where the marriage was concluded or where the defendant permanently resides or, by consent of the bishop of the defendant's place of residence and of the bishop of the locality of the preferred court and of its president, where the biggest part of the investigation has to be carried out. The bishops' conference can rule that a cleric may act as sole presiding judge, if there is no alternative. No restrictions are imposed on the right to appear as plaintiff. The same rights are assigned to legal counsel as to the *defensor vinculi*. A second suit is still required but is considerably abbreviated.

7. *Administrative Procedure*

The norms proposed for this relate to all administrative activities and procedures lying outside a judicial process, excepting those of the supreme authority. They also provide for an appeal against legislation by a lower authority. When it comes to administrative procedures the ruling body must be sure of having sufficient insight into the issues to be determined and the relevant evidence. The interested parties must be heard, unless this is obviously beside the point. Any person filing an application or appeal must be given opportunity to familiarize himself with the case and with the documentation, to reply to it and to call in the assistance of a lawyer or expert. The decision should be given in writing, with at least a summary statement of reasons. In all cases appeal to a higher authority remains open; one can turn to an administrative judge by reason of contravention of the law, misuse of authority or the giving of false reasons for a decision; to the ordinary judge, if one regards one's subjective rights as having been contravened. In the case of appeal against a decision by a bishop the higher authority, besides the Holy See, is a council of three bishops to be appointed by the national bishops' conference, which shall also nominate a court of three judges as an administrative court. A central court of final appeal for administrative jurisprudence is held to be desirable.

8. *Further Developments*

In his address to the Cardinals on 23 June 1970, Pope Paul VI informed them that the finished projects of the commission will first of all be submitted to the bishops, who in turn are to be the interpreters of the sense in these matters of the People of God. That consultation and the process of digesting it will certainly require a great deal of time; but for that very reason the legislation can be made more efficient and the time become ripe for a more fruitful reception of it (A.A.S. 62, 1970, p. 518). We may perhaps interpret these words in this sense: that after the more academic work of the commission's advisers the bishops and their advisers, clerical and lay, will have to assess what these proposals signify in practice, and to what extent they can be profitably carried out in the various countries. It was the commission's secretary, P. Raymundus Bidagor, s.j., who in May 1970, in a speech at the Institut Catholique in Paris, quoted the celebrated words of von Jhering: "The law—justice—exists only that it may be realized. This realization is the life and truth of the law. It is the law itself; what does not pass into reality, what exists only in legal enactments and on paper, is a mere shadow of justice, nothing but words". A realistic revision can only come about in a dialogue between theoretical knowledge and practice.

Translated by Hubert Hoskins

PART III
DOCUMENTATION
CONCILIUM

Giuseppe Alberigo Bologna

A Constitutional Law for the Church

WITH his letter of 10 February 1971, Cardinal Felici, in his capacity as President of the Commission for the Reform of Canon Law (CIC), sent all Roman Catholic bishops a bulky file containing the two most recent versions of the so-called Fundamental Law of the Church (*Lex ecclesiae fundamentalis*[1]), together with two explanatory reports prepared by W. Onclin, a canonist and secretary of the special Commission (*Commissio consultorum specialis*[2]) responsible for the drafts. The bishops were invited to give notice of acceptance or rejection by August.

I. A DECISIVE VOTE

The preparation of the draft Law and its recent dispatch to the bishops are marked by some distinctly interesting features. Indeed, all the editorial work has proceeded for some years with what might be called extreme circumspection within a small committee of experts which has prevented any information of any kind being leaked to the outside world. As Cardinal Felici's

[1] The *Textus prior* of September 1969 and the *Textus emendatus* of July 1970 have appeared already in the Bologna review *Il Regno* (1970, pp. 284–300; and 1971, pp. 112–19).

[2] The *Commissio consultorum specialis* was constituted in April 1967 (Pres.: Felici; Sec.: R. Bidagor and W. Onclin; Members: C. Colombo, Kl. Mörsdorf, C. Moeller, D. Faltin, W. Bertrams, P. Ciprotti, A. M. Charue, N. Jubany, M. Brini, I. Ziadé, A. del Portillo, E. Lanne). Despite the reasonably international composition of the Commission, its work has evidently been inspired by the Curia and directed towards a restoration of the past.

letter indicates, apart from the fleeting discussion at the Synod of 1967 nothing apparently occurred until in 1970 the draft known as the *Textus prior* was submitted to a restricted number of individuals: the cardinals of the Commission for the Reform of Canon Law, the advisers of the Congregation for Doctrine, and the members of the International Theological Commission.

This has meant that, with the exception of the 1967 Synod, there has been no collegial discussion of either the idea of or the text of the Law, and it would appear that members of collegial bodies have received the text only incidentally, as individuals. Of course there has been no real public debate of the documentation in question. There has not even been due deliberation by the Commission of cardinals charged with the reform of the CIC, which might well be considered the sole competent body in the formal sense. It would seem that the actual dissemination of the text among the bishops has replaced such reference to the Commission.

On the other hand, the letter of invitation to the bishops requiring them to answer two questions in regard to the draft Law is undoubtedly of a highly serious nature. It actually represents a consultation of the world episcopate, by which each bishop—as an individual or on behalf of his own episcopal conference—is asked to give a precise reply to the questions set him: the bishops have been summoned—no more and no less—to give a formal and final postal vote. This method would not really be problematical if the voting were preceded by an informed, full and public debate on the subject, and if the draft had been effectively made available for comment by and contributions from the episcopate and the Church. But that course has been neatly avoided, and cannot be adequately compensated for by one or two days of discussion in the Bishops' Conference.

The gravity of the vote requested is fully stressed in the above-mentioned letter from Cardinal Felici, where it is stated that each bishop should take care to give an *affirmative* or *negative* answer to the question whether it is expedient to make a *Lex ecclesiae fundamentalis*, for the whole Catholic Church, a law that would be the *theological and legal* basis for the various laws of the Church. In this regard *Relatio II* (pp. 122–123) refers to a document promulgating the Law, which would decree that all canon law would be interpreted in terms of the Law, and that any measures contrary to it would count as null and void. It is no exaggeration to stress how, in view of the foregoing, approval or rejection of the *Lex fundamentalis* is decisive, in the sense that it is destined to determine all future options for the Catholic Church, inasmuch as it constitutes the supreme criterion of its life and consequently an inevitable limitation of a plurality of charisms, and an impassable barrier for the dynamism of the community of the faithful and the responsibility of their pastors.

An attempt has been made to turn the vote required of the bishops into the world episcopate's sanctioning of the *Lex fundamentalis*, making it a formal decision of the episcopal College and quietly bypassing the question of the absence of any kind of debate. The postal vote is to be followed only by the Pope's approval and promulgation of the Law.

II. THE PEOPLE OF GOD UNDER THE LAW

The draft version of the Law consists of ninety-five canons, and a preface divided into three sections. The first is entitled "The Church or the People of God"; the second is concerned with the duties of the Church; and the third examines the relationship between the Church and human society. The structure of the draft is therefore clearly related to parts II and III of *Lumen Gentium*, and to *Gaudium et Spes*.

The preface and canons 1 and 2 deserve special attention, for in these texts the Law is presented and justified in its essential nature as a juridico-theological document. This aspect is clearly demonstrated in *Relatio I*: *"oportet ut (lex) proponat principia theologica structurae ecclesiae, atque exinde deducat normas iuridicas fundamentales quae pro omnibus vim habent"* (p. 64; cf. *Relatio II*, pp. 119 ff.).

In fact the preface is virtually a monograph on this very kind of deductive process. From the mission of the Son to the works of the Father (*"Aeternus Pater, qui Filium suum . . . misit"*, pref. I) a deduction is made regarding the mission of the Church (*"eique concredidit ut missionem qua ipse missus est . . . perduceret"*, pref. II), even concluding that the Church fulfils that mission (*"eam etiam implet"*) when it retains and guards its own divine constitution (obviously to be found first and foremost in the *Lex fundamentalis*): *"constitutionemque sibi divinitus impositam incolumen servat ac tutatur"*, pref. III). Likewise, there is a smooth transition from the Father's salvific will (*"credentes in Christum . . . convocare statuit in sanctam Ecclesiam"*, pref. I) to the institution of the Church as a hierarchical society as the work of Christ (*"Christus itaque Ecclesiam . . . societatem constituit hierarchicis organis instructam"*, pref. II); and that institution is made the basis and justification for the activity with which the Church, by way of its laws, guarantees the unity of the faith and preserves and defends its own constitution (pref. III). *Relatio II* states that in the Law *"affirmatur Evangelium esse fundamentum ecclesiae atque legum quae eiusdem constitutionem regunt"* (p. 131): the constitution and the laws of the Church can be traced back to the Gospel and derived from the Gospel.

What we in fact have is a deductive process in which the conclusions largely condition the premiss, in which the Gospel depends on the Law, and not vice versa. To be sure, considerable recourse is had to Vatican II for the matter of the *principia theologica structurae Ecclesiae*, but it is important to mark the difference of perspective (despite the irresolution and imperfection of the pronouncements cited from Vatican II). In *Lumen Gentium* the *principia theologica* (the Church as a mystery, the eschatological dimension, the idea of the community and of the People of God) establishes a vital and dynamic context in which the statements on the *structura Ecclesiae* are so placed and qualified as to take on new light and life; in the *Lex fundamentalis*, on the other hand, we find that a primary suasion is the attempt as far as possible to guarantee an absolutization of the juridical code, which of its very nature already tends to rigidity. Hence the tendency of the deductive process to allow conclusions on the legal level to affect the premisses: the court to which the Law is subject as a canonical document is conceived after the model of the constitutional law of the sovereign state. This is clearly evident: there is an insistence on a definitive ruling, on absoluteness, on certitude, on uniformity, on organic completeness, on precise definition, and on the necessity of knowing unequivocally what the Church is, and what or who does and does not appertain or belong to it.

This kind of reductive operationism is displayed throughout the document in question. Attention is called to it in every feature. Above all we find a reference to the idea of the Church as *sacramentum seu signum et instrumentum* at the end of the preface pt. II, where it is defined as a *societas hierarchicis organis instructa* invested with the mission entrusted to it by Christ, devoid of the dimension of the Church as mystery to be found in *Lumen Gentium* 1; the Church according to the *Lex fundamentalis* is not a symbol or sign which refers to the transcendence and sovereignty of God, but exists as a perfectly articulated organism, which is indeed now and henceforward self-sufficient, wholly in possession of its own self-consciousness and capable of objectifying it in a constitutional law. The eschatological prediction of the Kingdom which should make the human institution an object for discussion appears as an assured possession of the Church, which is the irrefragable and definitive plenipotentiary (cf. can. 1.1: *"societatem hierarchice ordinatam ... ad regnum Dei ... ulterius in hoc mundo dilatandum"*). It can be seen why *Relatio I* refuses to allow the provisional character of the *Lex fundamentalis*, stating instead that the *"affirmatio indolis provisoriae ansam praeberet incertitudini iuridicae"* (p. 64). In this context, the call for *perennis reformatio* of the pilgrim Church and the requirement *ut unum sint* (which occurs in can. 2.4 of the *Textus emendatus*) are plainly redundant, given the absence of any indication of relevant criteria and of means for renewal.

Particular attention should be paid to the theme of the Church as a theandric organism. It recurs in *De liturgia* (n. 2), in the context of an affirmation of the primacy of the cultic and spiritual function of the Church, and is to be found in *Lumen Gentium* in the description of the doctrine of the mysterious-sacramental nature of the Church (n. 8). In the *Lex fundamentalis* there is an affirmation of the complex divine-human nature of the ecclesial organism but there is a significant shift of the emphasis on the terms: the visible, active, juridical, actual human element is justified, guaranteed and absolutized by the divine element, so that in the Law *"identitas elucet inter Ecclesiam charismatis et Ecclesiam iuris"* (*Relatio I*, p. 70). In short, the notion of the

People of God, which in the conciliar statement is introduced so as positively to disarrange the ecclesiological *status quo*, loses its very innovative force. The appeal to the historical and eschatological dimension, the affirmation of the unity and the equality of the faithful, and the particular nature of the People of God among all other people, are all elements which disappear in the static conformism of the juridical letter of the *Lex fundamentalis*. According to the text: *"Christi Ecclesia est novus Dei populus, communitas spiritualis fidelium quae his in terris in societatem hierarchice ordinatam constituta est"* (can. 1.1); the notions of the People of God, of the *Ecclesia*, of *communitas*, and of *societas* are made comparable and placed on a lower level. In particular, the concept of the People of God is interpreted reductively: what we have is an inverse relation of the People of God to the Church, compared with that in *Lumen Gentium* 9, where on the contrary the notion of the Church is inherent in that of the People of God which takes on an eschatological significance. The affirmation of the common priesthood in can. 1.2 is designed, by means of a sacral and hieratic interpretation of the concept of "people", to advance the distinction between the people and the *"ministri qui sacra qua instruuntur potestate deputantur ut in persona Christi et Eius auctoritate sint pastores ..."* (can. 1.3). The function of the Spirit, in accordance with the whole tendency of the document, is no more than that of guaranteeing the possession of truth by the institutional order: *"ecclesiam quam in omnem ventatem inducit, diversis donis hierarchicis et charismaticis ordinate instruit et dirigit"* (can. 1.4).

In the same chap. I various canons are inserted (14, 16, 17, 23) which are intended to safeguard the rights of Christians, but on examination not only their essentially ephemeral character becomes clear, but the possibility of their conversion into oppressive norms in the hands of those who wield ecclesiastical power. As for the hierarchy of truths, a comparison of *De Oecumenismo* n. 11 and can. 9 and 57 reveals a complete reversal of the conciliar declaration. Likewise, in regard to the assertion of religious liberty, can. 5, 19, 88 and 89 substantially modify the teaching of *Dignitatis humanae*.[3]

[3] Cf. P. G. Camaiani, "La *Lex ecclesiae fundamentalis* e la libertà religiosa", IDOC, May 1971.

III. Towards the Restoration of the Vertical Church

As a whole, article 2 of chap. I of the Law—*De hierarchia in ecclesia constituta* (can. 31–50)—offers itself as a parallel to chap. III of *Lumen Gentium*. In reality the analogy is limited almost wholly to abundant material use of the texts of *Lumen Gentium*. It is in fact easy to see that the use made of the sources is entirely unscrupulous in regard to the overall economy and logic of the conciliar constitution—in short, to its theology. Therefore, while not disregarding the considerable limitations of *Lumen Gentium* —whether in terms of the balance between the first and second chapters on the one hand and third on the other, or in respect to the further development of the ecclesial consciousness which has taken place in the last few years—it is interesting and indeed decisive to analyse this part of the draft *Lex fundamentalis* from the viewpoint of the conciliar constitution.

In this context there is a levelling-down of the texts, by means of which the canons are larded with expressions taken from documents substantially diverse and disparate in theological qualification, historical reference and theological orientation; it is not difficult to detect the significance of this ploy: there are frequent additions or omissions within scraps of texts from the conciliar decisions: in short, we have a forced use of conciliar statements within a theological schema quite different from that of *Lumen Gentium*.

Direct evidence of this procedure is to be found in the difference between the ecclesiology of Vatican II and that of the draft *Lex fundamentalis*. The Law disregards the order in which arguments are presented. The presentation found in the Law retains the parallelism of the initial and final sections (can. 31–33: the divine institution of the ministries in the Church, and 49–50: the priesthood and diaconate), but the draft would seem to have discarded any due and proper treatment of the argument as it appears in *Lumen Gentium*. It begins with the canons on the supreme pontiff (34–36), which it follows with those on the institution of bishops (37–38), the episcopal College (39–40), the ecumenical Council (41–46), the bishops as such (47–48), and then the priests and deacons (49–50). The result is that the canons on the Pope are isolated from the main body of the teaching on the episcopate, and thus treated first, and outside the context of the episcopal College; and that the sections dedicated to the episcopal College and to the ecumenical Council are formally separated from the section on the Pope and made part of par. 2, *De episcopis*.

The schema of the draft Law is substantially extraneous and contrary to that of *Lumen Gentium*, and is not in accordance with that of CIC, for it presents a conception of the ecclesial hierarchy which is incredibly centralized and verticalist. The treatment of the Roman pontiff in a section entirely separate from and without reference to that on the ecumenical Council is evidence of the implicitly dualistic and contrary nature of the ideology of the document.

The obstructive effect of such a document in regard to ecumenism is evident despite the *sollicitudo de oecumenismo* claimed by *Relatio II* (pp. 125–126). It is impossible to allow the *Lex* any just claim to an essentially "universalistic" ecclesiological perspective when it does not recognize the essential freedom of local churches and a pluralism of their experiences and charisms. It is paradoxical when one recalls that, at the Synod of bishops in 1967, Felici defended the necessity of the Law as a guarantee of two distinct codices for the Latin and the Oriental Churches.

Chap. II—*De ecclesiae muneribus* (can. 51–83)—is intended to act as the pivot for all the canonical summaries regarding the Church, and uses the theme of the *munera* of Christ: priesthood, kingship and prophecy. The draft follows this division proficiently, but so as to present the existing situation as in conformity with the will of Christ himself, while excluding any instance of reform. The gifts of Christ are not there for the reform of the Church; instead, the *status quo* of the Western Roman Church of the nineteen-seventies is to become the sole (grotesque) authorized realization of Christ's *munera*.

In addition, in the section cited, the *Lex fundamentalis* lacks any pneumatology (cf. can. 51.1), that is, a genuine and exact trinitarian theology. Brief references to the Spirit are inserted in the *Textus emendatus*, but serve only to confirm this lack, inasmuch as no change is made in the structure or design of the chapter. No less serious is the fact that the Christology of the *Lex fundamentalis* does not acknowledge the distinction between the earthly Christ and the glorified Christ, and between the functions of the one and the other; it is wholly without a theology of the crucified Christ and, all the more, its relation to the character of the Church. Consequently, the lack of any proper acknowledgment of the pilgrim Church depends on a definite theological lacuna. The presuppositions of the Law also display a lack of any theology of the Word. On the one hand, in fact, in the *"munus docendi"* to which the Law refers, there is no primary and exact reference to *"praedicare Evangelium"*. On the other hand, it is remarked that the word *"docere"* is not only different from *"praedicare Evangelium"*, but, in the acceptation peculiar to the *Lex fundamentalis*, it is in no way reducible to the teaching—the *didascalia* which in Jesus, then in his apostles and beyond them in the Church as well, has a fundamental place next to the kerygma.

From the ecclesiological viewpoint, the Church is not distinct from the Kingdom of God; in the same chapter, there is no acknowledgment of the dimension of mystery, pilgrimage and eschatology of the Church. The Church is conceived as a *societas* rather than as a *communitas*; consequently the global investment of the *munera* cannot be individually articulated. The *munera* are substantially unique. The ecclesiology of communion is as good as denied and suppressed.

In the same perspective, the *munus regendi* (art. 3) in the *Lex fundamentalis* is a function of a Church conceived as a society and not as a *communitas spiritualis*. The fact that the Law, in contradistinction to *Lumen Gentium*, does not make any proficient distinction between the Church and the Kingdom, leads to a conception of the *munus regendi* that rests upon a highly problematical definition. In fact it would seem difficult to distinguish the nature of the authority which, according to this conception, is exercised by the Church, from that which the Father exercises in the Kingdom. Furthermore, authority is conceived as an emphatically centralized form individualized in the person of the Pope. The Pope and the College are conceived in a clearly antagonistic way (cf. can. 76). Notwithstanding the reference in can. 40, in practice there is no allowance for true and proper forms of the exercise of *munus regendi* by the episcopal College; the complete absence of any reference whatsoever to the ecumenical Council may be taken as indicative of this tendency!

In can. 75.2, the *munus regendi* is expressed in terms of the threefold legislative, executive and juridical power dear to liberal constitutionalism. But, apart from the absurdity of applying to a reality *sui generis* such as the Church a temporally and locally circumscribed political schema, the constitutionalism to which the *Lex fundamentalis* refers is neatly restricted to a formal expression without any provision for the conditions and organs capable of guaranteeing the aforesaid threefold division and the consequent liberty of the *subditi*. Can. 33 removes any remaining illusion in this regard. Furthermore, the design of the *Lex fundamentalis* evidences a desire to return—by means of the anachronistic confusion between the Christological *munera* and the three powers dear to Montesquieu—to the division between *ordo* and *jurisdictio*, which—as is well known—was overcome by Vatican II.

IV. The Goal of the Fundamental Law

In section III—*De Ecclesia et hominum consortione* (can. 84–95)—the schema, compared with that of the two preceding sections, is still more distant from the spirit of the documents of Vatican II, and gives the impression of being the real expression of the true intention of the *Lex fundamentalis*: namely, a reduction of the Church to a *societas* which is legally constituted and has its own individuality, rights and privileges, and above all enjoys a position in its own right among all other sovereign orders in the world. *Relatio II* (p. 155) makes clear that the rights and liberty claimed on behalf of the Church are to be interpreted as privileges in ideological and theologico-juridical terms which were positively and fundamentally refuted by the documents of Vatican II. A reading of canons 84–95 reinforces this impression, and shows that the very nucleus of the *Lex fundamentalis* is actually to be found in the more juridical section which is much more explicit in its refutation of the mystery of the Church.

One of the major inadequacies of this chapter consists in the use of the term "Church" with connotations which are significantly different from, and for the most part extraneous to, the New Testament, despite the affirmation to the contrary in *Relatio II* (pp. 121, 144). The qualifications of can. 84.2 and 93 are contradicted by those of can. 86, by which *ecclesia* is set against *sub-ditos*, and those of can. 9.41, where *ecclesia* and *fideles* are two distinct entities; in addition, *ecclesia* signifies the Holy See in the canons which treat of its international juridical character (95.1), or the possession of material goods (92; 94.4). For the most part, *ecclesia* is identified with *societas*, which is difficult to reconcile with the interpretation of *ecclesia* as the People of God.

In the same canons 84–95, despite the reference to *Gaudium et Spes* (especially nn. 40, 42 and 76), the fundamental concepts of the conciliar document are frequently contradicted. Above all, everything that *Gaudium et Spes* (n. 40) explicitly says about Vatican II's view of the mystery of the Church ("presupposing everything which has already been said by this Council concerning the mystery of the Church") is absent from the *Lex funda: mentalis*. Especially significant is the inadequacy of the theological premiss, as is apparent on comparing the preface to *Gaudium et Spes*, which talks of *"Communitas . . . Christi discipulorum"* and of *"nuntium salutis omnibus proponendum"*, with can. 84.1 of the *Lex fundamentalis*. Here the terms of the dialogue have become both rigidified and simplified: the world is reduced to *societates, consortii* whose importance is directly proportional to their legal consistency and their power, whereas the preface to *Gaudium et Spes* speaks of *"mundum hominum seu universam familiam humanam"* and it is significant that the paragraph cited most often (five times) from *Gaudium et Spes* is in fact n. 76, which refers to the relations between the political community and the Church. In relation to this political society, the Church, identified with a hierarchically ordered (can. 94.1) *societas* of a particular type is placed in a position of parity, with an international juridical character and a number of rights to affirm. It is significant that the *Lex fundamentalis*, when citing *Gaudium et Spes*, replaces *servitium* with *munus* (can. 86.2), *gravissimum officium* with *ius* (can. 91), and even *competit* with *debet* (can. 94.3), and so on. It is not so much a case of stylistic substitution as of the replacement of concepts found inadequate by reason of their incompatibility with the ecclesiology of the *Lex fundamentalis*. An ecclesiastical *societas* is not made to serve other *societates* (even though *Gaudium et Spes* 42 states *"De adiutorio quo Ecclesia societati humanae afferre satagit"*, but above all to maintain self-affirmation. The affirmation of rights is so dominant a concern that little cognizance is taken of the fact that *Relatio I* states, in regard to chapter III, that in the *Lex fundamentalis* "*definiuntur ... obligationes et iura ecclesiae ipsius*" (p. 113).

The difficult dialogue which, albeit with some vagueness, *Gaudium et Spes* posited as necessary between the Church and the world is reduced here to a relationship between two *societates*, both standing for their respective *subditi*. In this way the Church is defined as a society distinct from the other *societates* which compose the world; but this distinction does not consist in the fact that the Church is a mystery, in which case it would not be distinct but different, but more in the fact that the Church claims to have rights in regard to all other human societies, and title to, for example, the possession of goods, the media of social communication, privileges and a legal individuality. Of course the juridical formulation does not admit that participation in the joys and sorrows of the world that was asserted as the primary and better motive of *Gaudium et Spes*. Hence the *Lex fundamentalis* does not keep faith with what *Gaudium et Spes* 42 states in regard to the force of the Church, which does not consist "*in dominio aliquo externo mediis mere humanis exercendo*" ("For the force which the Church can inject into the modern society of man consists in that faith and charity put into vital practice, not in any external dominion exercised by merely human means"), but is concerned with the nature of supreme sovereignty, juridical individuality, and the possession of material goods, all of which are vigorously laid claim to. Similarly, there is no evidence of the disavowal of hope in privileges and the readiness to renounce the exercise of certain legitimately acquired rights which were expressly affirmed by Vatican II (*Gaudium et Spes* 76).

The main source of this last group of canons is indeed Vatican II, but for the most part interpreted almost wholly in a more reductive manner, by which the implications of the Council are toned down on the pretext of excluding questions which are intended to be left open (cf. can. 94.1 in regard to the translation of bishops).

V. An Overall Evaluation of the Schema

If we try to summarize the elements which have emerged from an analysis of the whole draft—based on a systematic examination carried out by the Institute for Religious Science of Bologna —we may conclude that the theological structure represents an attempt to express juridically a Christian ecclesiology that implies a renunciation of the very pivot of that ecclesiology: the mystery of the Church, its dependence on the Trinity, the pilgrim and dynamic and unceasingly penitential aspect of its life, the effective interaction between the local communities and the universal Church, the incessant search for more adequate forms of expression for its intimate reality of prayer, communion and charity, its ultimate co-extensiveness with the Eucharist, its search for unity in faith and in liberty. All these points are essentially absent from and extraneous to the schema of the *Lex fundamentalis*, but are requisite to any truly proficient effort of this kind. It is not a question of the pride or defective intention of the editors, but of the radical defectiveness of the very idea of a constitutional law of the Church which is not more susceptible to adequate and faithful drafting.

The logic of the draft results in additional contradiction. The illusion that it is possible to do injury to logic and legal language in order to express the profound reality of the Church is accompanied by a subordination of that reality to rigid juridical requirements; the ultimate effect is a radical secularization of the Church, which is reduced to its human historico-institutional and temporal elements. This is not to deny the constant occurrence in the draft of the *Lex fundamentalis* of declarations regarding the divine origin of the Church, on which its life and structure are said to depend. In reality, however, the above examination will have shown that there is a typical reversal of connotation by virtue of which the theological affirmations do not govern the economy of the Law, but, on the contrary, that function is performed by the concrete propositions relating to its structure. Consequently, the external movement of the discourse is deduced from the *principia theologica* in order to relate to the statements on the *structura ecclesiae*, but in substance it is those statements and the actual existing institutional order which condition the premisses and deprive them of adequate logical foundation. Analogously, the structure of the *Lex fundamentalis* is such as to allow apparent precedence to the first part, whereas in fact the sections on hierarchy and the Church as a secular power govern the rest of the document.

Hence the attempt to base the canonistic treatise on the three functions—kingship, priesthood and prophecy—of Christ results in a concealment of the perspective of the Kingdom. The affirmation of the Church as the People of God, as a community of the faithful, is contradicted and refuted by an exclusively individualistic interpretation in terms of rights and structure. Hence it may only too easily be predicted that if such a *Lex fundamentalis* were approved, it would be used to control a rigidly deductive drafting of particular codices, thus denying spontaneity, adaptability and pluralism.

With regard to method, it is essential to note the way in which the draft of the *Lex fundamentalis* has been produced, and particularly the multitude of references which the editors have thought necessary to include in the notes. The decisions of Vatican II, however, are cited according to a rigid logic that is not that of the conciliar documents. The structure of the draft is preordained, and the conciliar extracts—or, rather, fragments—which happen to accord with the set form have been inserted one by one. When it has been impossible to find single extracts which would fit a canon, shreds have been torn from various conciliar sources without due attention to the varying contexts, so that they attain now to a meaning other than that allowed them by the Council. Individual phrases are also quoted which the conciliar documents had cited from other sources (CIC, papal encyclicals, Vatican I), or radical alterations are made to the mode of citation employed in the texts of Vatican II. In this way the draft avoids proper citation of the conciliar texts and presents canons which are wholly foreign in form and content to Vatican II. A notable fault is the absence of Scriptural quotations. In this regard, *Relatio II* (p. 125) states that recourse is not had to the Bible in the *Lex fundamentalis* because it has of its nature to use *"modus dicendi disciplinae iuridicae proprius"*. The explanation is illuminating in its implicit acknowledgment of the impossibility of formulating an *imago ecclesiae* (*ibid.*, p. 119) in a constitutional law which on principle renounces biblical language.

The *Lex fundamentalis* has been drafted with what might be called total liberty in regard to Vatican II, and the broad use of material drawn from the conciliar texts should not be allowed to conceal the substantial distance between the Law and the teaching of the Council. There is no doubt that Gasparri was incomparably more faithful to the preceding legislation in 1917 in the drafting of the CIC than the drafters of the *Lex fundamentalis* to the decisions of Vatican II.

The language of the *Lex fundamentalis* also features modifications which are symptomatic of its whole tendency. *Societas* replaces *communitas*, *veritas* supplants *fides*, *officium* appears in place of *onus*, *potestas* or *munus* is used rather than *servitium*, *ius* replaces *officium*. No less indicative of a transposition which is increasingly tantamount to falsification are the modifications introduced in the significance of key-words. *Ecclesia*, for example, no longer denotes *ecclesia ab Abel* (*Lumen Gentium*, 2.25), *templum Spiritus* (*Lumen Gentium*, 4.49), *ecclesia exul* (*Lumen Gentium*, 6.117); it rarely stands for the community of the faithful, and much more frequently is a synonym for *societas*, and for *potestas, hierarchia, auctoritas* or the Holy See. In addition, when *ecclesia* effectively denotes *populus Dei*, the mistaken equation of the *ecclesia* and therefore of the People of God with the Roman Catholic Church remains. *Eucharistia, subditos, christifideles*, and so on, suffer from analogous errors.

VI. A "Lex fundamentalis" is impossible and unacceptable

So serious an enterprise requires special attention; it is increasingly evident that it is not a question of amending the draft version of the Law,[4] but of realizing that the very idea of a constitutional law of the Church is unacceptable and must be met with

---

[4] The sequence of *textus prior* and *textus emendatus* has not resulted in any effective improvement in the structure of the Law. The refusal of the editorial Commission to take into consideration most of the observations received clearly shows the complete absence of flexibility, and therefore of adaptability of the genus "constitution" to the requirements of ecclesial reality.

a plain refusal. A careful reading of the draft shows the qualitative impossibility, and the really chimerical or dangerously mystifying nature of the illusive attempt to prepare a constitutional charter for the Church—an attempt originating, significantly, within the Roman Curia in an obvious bid to restore the ecclesiology dominant before Vatican II. That ecclesiology was rejected in Council by the vast majority of the bishops of the Church. An undertaking like the *Lex fundamentalis* was neither evident, nor even conceived or attempted for nearly two thousand years; not, to be sure, because of any lack of imagination or cultural refinement, but because of an informed awareness that the constitutive and fundamental nucleus of the Church (*status ecclesiae*, as they said in the Middle Ages) cannot be adequately formulated with the instruments of legal science, by reason of their schematic, one-dimensional, positive and systematic nature—which is of value to the Church, but only in the case of specific and concrete statutes (*statuta ecclesiae*).

The thesis, put about in the last few years, of the need for a theologization, or even a "sacramentalization", of canon law indicates the limitations and immaturity of the propositions. To give the Church a "constitution" does not mean the organic development of canon law that has accompanied the Church throughout its life, but implies, on the contrary, a novelty foreign to ecclesial tradition. A rejection of the *Lex fundamentalis* is not a denial of the ecclesial legitimacy of canon law. It is an expression of the conviction that the essence of the Church and the ultimate criteria of its life and its structure transcend such attempts at legal formulation, which will inevitably result in ossification and falsification.

It is absolutely necessary that there should be a full discussion both in and outside the Catholic Church; otherwise the "constitutional" enterprise may well result in an argument that will seriously injure Church life. The action of the bishops should be to ensure that the question is adjourned for some years and submitted to a proficient debate that would adequately express the true consciousness of the Church.

Translated by Verdant Green

Biographical Notes

TISSA BALASURIYA, O.M.I., was born 29 August 1924 in Ceylon and was ordained in 1952. He studied at the Universities of Ceylon, Rome, Oxford and Paris. Licentiate in philosophy and theology, with a diploma in economy, he is rector of the Aquinas University College, Ceylon. He has written various articles on liberty and authority, on ecumenism, Communism in Asia, etc.

RUUD J. BUNNIK was born 10 February 1932 in Amersfoort (Netherlands) and was ordained in 1957. He studied at the University of Nijmegen. He teaches English at the Seminary of Apeldoorn (Netherlands) and is a member of the editorial board of *Septuagintes*. He has written notable contributions on a new theology of the ministry, on the celibacy of priests, on priestly vocation and the seminary, etc.

GIOVANNI CAPRILE, S.J., was born in 1917 in Portici (Italy). Licentiate in philosophy and theology, he is contributor to *Civiltà Cattolica* on the present religious state. Among his published works are: *Il Concilio Vaticano II* (6 vols.) and two volumes of documentation on the Synod of Bishops (1967 and 1969).

MAXWELL CHARLESWORTH was born 30 December 1925 in Victoria (Australia), and is a Catholic. He studied at the Universities of Melbourne, Louvain and London. Master of arts, doctor of philosophy, he is reader in philosophy at the University of Melbourne and lay consultor to the Secretariat for Non-Believers. Among his published works are: *Athéisme et philosophie analytique* (1970) and *The Problem of Religious Language* (1971).

MARIE-DOMINIQUE CHENU, O.P., was born 7 January 1895 in Paris and was ordained in 1918. He studied at the Angelicum (Rome). Doctor of theology he has taught the history of theology at the Faculties of the Saulchoir (France) and was a professor at the Sorbonne. Among his publications are: *Pour une théologie du travail* (Paris, 1955; republished 1965) and *Peuple de Dieu dans le monde* (Paris, 1966).

GUSTAVO GUTIERREZ was born 8 June 1928 in Lima and was ordained in 1959. He studied at the University of Louvain and at the Catholic Faculties of Lyons. Licentiate in psychology and theology, he is professor of theology and social sciences at the Catholic University of Lima, and national assessor of the National Union of Catholic Students. Among his published works are: *La pastoral de la Iglesia latinoamericana* (Montevideo, 1968) and *Apuntes para una Teología de la Liberación* (Lima, 1971).

KARL-BEHRND HASSELMAN was born in 1933 in Hamburg and is a Lutheran. He has made higher studies in philosophy and theology. He is pastor of students and of a Lutheran community in Flensburg (Germany). Among his published works is *Politische Gemeinde, ein kirchliches Handlungsmodell am Beispiel der Evangelischen Studentengemeinde an der Freien Universität Berlin* (Hamburg, 1969).

PETER HUIZING, S.J., was born 22 January 1911 in Haarlem (Netherlands) and ordained in 1942. He studied at the Universities of Amsterdam, Nijmegen, Louvain, Munich and at the Gregorian (Rome). Licentiate in philosophy and theology, doctor of civil law and canon law, he is professor of canon law and of the history of canon law at the University of Nijmegen; he is also consultor of the Roman Commission for the revision of the Code of Canon Law. Among his published works is *De Trentse huwelijksvorm* (Hilversum/Antwerp, 1966).

PEDRO LOMBARDIA was born 14 July 1930 in Cordova (Spain) and is a Catholic. He studied at the Universities of Granada, Madrid and St Thomas (Rome). Doctor of civil law and canon law, he is professor of canon law at the University of Navarre, editor of the review *Ius Canonicum* and consultor of the Roman Commission for the revision of the Code of Canon Law. He has written several articles on the laity and law in the Church, on canon law in the life of the Church, on the *Lex fundamentalis*, etc.

PAUL PHILIBERT, O.P., was born 30 December 1936 in Baltimore and was ordained in 1963. He is professor of moral theology at Providence College, Rhode Island, and lecturer on liturgical celebration and music. He has written notable articles on the theology of the religious life in the modern world, on an epistemology of the faith, etc.

EMILE JEAN PIN was born 2 December 1921 in Lyons. He studied at the Universities of Grenoble, Montpellier, Paris, Lyons and Chicago. Licentiate in law and in theology, docteur ès lettres (sociology), he is a professor of sociology (general sociology and sociology of religion). Among his published works are: *Pratiques religieuses et Classes sociales* (Paris, 1956), *Les Classes sociales* (Paris, 1962) and (in collaboration with Hervé Carrier) *Essais de sociologie religieuse* (Paris, 1967).

HANS VAN PINXTEREN, M.H.M., was born 4 July 1918 in Rosmalen (Netherlands) and was ordained in 1942. He studied at the University of Nijmegen, at Maestricht and at the Gregorian (Rome). Doctor of theology, he is reader in missiology at the University of Nijmegen and lecturer to the Association for contacts between the continents at Soesterberg. He has written various articles on missiology.

GERHARD SCHNEIDER was born 15 June 1926 in Treves and was ordained in 1952. He studied in Treves and Munich. Doctor of theology, he is professor of New Testament at the University of Bochum (Germany). Among his published works are: *Der Herr, unser Gott. Zur Biblischen Gottesverkündidigung* (Stuttgart, 1965) and *Studien zur lukanischen Darstellung der Passion* (Munich, 1969).